A FINDS MANUAL

EXCAVATING, PROCESSING & STORING

To Lucy + Brian,

Lots of love

Naveena

D1422219

A FINDS MANUAL
EXCAVATING, PROCESSING & STORING

NORENA SHOPLAND

TEMPUS

This book is dedicated to Juls
With all my love and all my thanks

First published 2006

Tempus Publishing Limited
The Mill, Brimscombe Port,
Stroud, Gloucestershire, GL5 2QG
www.tempus-publishing.com

© Norena Shopland, 2006

The right of Norena Shopland to be identified as the Author
of this work has been asserted in accordance with the
Copyrights, Designs and Patents Act 1988.

British Library Cataloguing in Publication Data.
A catalogue record for this book is available from the British Library.

ISBN 0 7524 3588 4

Typesetting and origination by Tempus Publishing Limited
Printed in Great Britain

CONTENTS

INTRODUCTION

The term 'find' refers to portable objects recovered from an archaeological excavation; as a result of metal detecting; as a stray find from field walking; or as a casual find. The word portable can refer to items which would not be considered easy to move; for example, statuary of any size is regarded as a find. Even something as large as the medieval ship the *Mary Rose* (which was recovered from the Solent and needed a crane to lift it from the water) is still defined and treated as a find.

The majority of finds recovered from an archaeological excavation are fragmentary and may on first sight appear to be of no real importance. However one scruffy, battered sherd can turn out to be a type of pot never previously found in the country. This is the basis behind the edict that all finds should be regarded as valuable – particularly as so many objects do not even make it into the archaeological record. Decay will remove many items within a few years of deposition and valuable items are rarely deposited.

Those items which do make it into the archaeological record are subject to a number of vagaries. The primary position of the piece may be altered by natural and cultural interference (Chapter 1), resulting in artefacts being moved into secondary positions which require more complex analysis and interpretation of the site.

Other considerations are more mundane. Modern archaeology is dependent on the 'Polluter Pays Principle' – those developers who wish to build upon a given piece of ground must pay for the archaeology. Developers who are generally up against a time constraint themselves do not, on the whole, like archaeology to hold up their schedule. This is particularly true when an area is due to be handed over by the archaeologists as, of course, the greatest finds are commonly made on the afternoon of the last day before handover. The author was on a site where a pit designed to hold live fish and oysters was uncovered, revealing rare delft tiles. As the development was held up there was bad feeling between the excavation team and the construction workers who decided to attempt sabotage. Obviously this was counter-productive as the pit still had to be excavated but it shows how much archaeologists and their work can be disliked.

A more worrying aspect is the confidentiality clause which means the developer can refuse not only to have the archaeological report published but prevent anyone, even finds specialists, from looking at the reports. This control by those who may find archaeology a nuisance is a matter of concern.

Competitive tendering for the rights to excavate sites forces units to bid against each other. This process drives prices ever lower, meaning less money to carry out the work and so fewer staff, time, resources, finds specialists and conservators – and less time to publish the report. Diggers are employed on very short-term, often weekly, contracts, pay is poor, there is no career structure within a unit and consequently there is a high turnover of personnel. It is therefore understandable that diggers may not always want to engage in any form of responsibility. Once finds are recovered it is often cheaper not to have them processed but to store them instead. Therefore units and museums end up with collections stored for long periods of time (see Chapter 9) with no attention paid to them, so that certain more unstable items can decay (see Chapter 6) and be lost – making it a waste of time to excavate them in the first place. If the unit has run out of money the report on those finds which have been studied may never be published. This lack of publication means that nothing is added to the nationwide database and so studies are held back. Regional knowledge is particularly affected as incoming archaeology units may be unable to determine what is important to the area and little information coming out will not improve local knowledge.

Even when taking all these considerations into account, finds still have to go through the excavation itself, with all its particular vagaries (see Chapter 2). Finds recovery is dependent in many ways on the ability (or lack of it) of the excavator, not only in relation to their experience but also in their attitude towards collecting, as some excavators will collect every little scrap, where others will not. Collection may be beyond the digger's control as many finds are hard to see. Roman Samian pottery, thanks to its shiny red colour, has a high recovery rate, and gold, copper and other metals can be seen due to their noticeable colour. Large pieces cannot often be missed either, but items such as dark coloured pottery which blends with the soil can often be overlooked, as can items encrusted in dirt – metal detectorists working on a site will often find coins in the spoil heap which have been missed by the diggers.

Contextual archaeology has improved the general recording of archaeology; however, in relation to finds it can cause difficulties. Finds are split up according to their context no matter what their relationship may have been on the ground, and reports are compiled individually, splitting the finds up once more.

Effective recovery of finds is important for a number of reasons. Not only are they the things the public want to see on display in museums, but they are vital as the backbone of the dating system. Finds can indicate the status of an individual, the economy of a site and the trade-route patterns of antiquity. Even those items which have no known trade route can be traced back petrologically (the method of examining the material construction of a piece and comparing it to similar materials around the world) to try to discover its source. Even then it may be difficult to know what is being traded, the artefact itself or the material. An example of this is the tracing of some British Neolithic axes. It is not known if the axes themselves were traded or the blanks. Knowing one way or the other would throw enormous light on manufacture.

Artefacts can have meanings beyond our knowledge. What to us may be a mundane object may to others be a luxury item. We are also brought up to regard certain items in certain ways. In the western psyche flint tools belong to the prehistoric era; however, Australian aboriginals were using flint tools only a few hundred years ago. The three age system of Thomsen – Stone Age, Bronze Age and Iron Age, breaks down when compared to modern cultures. The use of anthropology to draw parallels with ancient civilisations is also loaded with dangers. No matter how close their material culture may seem, the attitudes towards their objects is probably entirely different. The world has moved on since the pre-historic era and the history of many cultures cannot be known, so any comparison is loaded with potential assumptions.

The study of finds in relation to a site is a linear process of recovery: processing; specialist analysis; interpretation; and publication. This can lead to collections being divorced not only in contextual recording but when sent to individual finds specialists. There is an ideal — for example, Catalhoyuk in Turkey. This site has a non-linear approach, with a specifically designed computerised system to which all involved add on a regular basis. Such knowledge sharing allows all members of the team to access any information available about the area they are working in. Specialists publish their reports and anyone uncovering a find can carry out a comparative study. They have a dedicated website with public forums enabling everyone to have a voice — even those whose interpretations are not so widely accepted. However, Catal Hoyuk (in Turkey) is a well-funded site with a high reputation and many are eager to work on it, unlike many other current archaeological excavations.

In the present archaeological climate much of the finds processing is done by volunteers or diggers doubling up as processors. This is not an ideal situation as many of these people are not experienced in the iden-tification of materials, let alone the finds themselves. The proper care of artefacts is often compromised. When reviewing the titles of archaeolog-ical books, none are dedicated solely to the care of finds and entries in general excavation volumes are often so scant they take up only a couple of pages. This book is an attempt to address that deficit.

1

STRATIGRAPHY AND SOILS

Stratigraphy is the study of the layers of the earth that are normally chronologically ordered with the earliest at the bottom. Each stratum differs from the one above and below in texture (the size of soil particles), chemical composition, types of inclusions, colour, thickness and archaeological features/finds, and they are rarely uniform. In geology rock layers are dated by inclusions such as fossils and by radio isotope dating. In archaeology it is the objects (excluding intrusions) and features found within a layer that provide the date. Artefacts and features which have no date will be dated by the layer, which in turn was dated by other already dated artefacts/features. In an ideal world a stratigraphic section would be a series of sealed layers dated by the artefacts and features they contain. However, this rarely happens as most layers are not sealed but reworked by natural and anthropogenic activities. This 'muddling up' of the artefacts and features can move them not just within their originating layer but to a completely different place from where they started. It is unravelling this disturbance of the stratigraphy that allows an analysis of the activities in that area, and to do this it is useful to have some understanding of how soils work.

Stratigraphy

The basic stratigraphic sequence consists of:

Ground level
Topsoil Largely composed of leaf litter, fine mineral particles, stones and dead matter that has been transformed into 'humus'.

Subsoil the main body of subsoil is low in humus compared to the top-soil, although there is some residue in the uppermost layer. Nutrients and minerals are washed down into the subsoil and the roots of plants gather these along with the water that sits between the soil particles.

Weathered parent material Mainly consisting of rock particles, there is little organic material in this level, which can be very deep. The level may also contain rocks moved from elsewhere due to glacial movement.

Bedrock As well as covered with the soil layers bedrock can be exposed and sometimes shows evidence of manufacturing activities such as the Iron Age and Roman querns from the Bristol area.

TABLE I SOIL GRADES

British Standards Institute Scale of Soil Grades		
		Size in mm
Stones or cobbles		Greater than 60
Gravel		60 – 20
Sand	coarse	2.0 – 0.6
	medium	0.6 – 0.2
	fine	0.2 – 0.06
Silt	coarse	0.06 – 0.02
	medium	0.02 – 0.006
	fine	0.006 – 0.002
Clay		less than 0.002

SOILS

The soils that exist between the parent rock and ground level in different zones vary according to weathering and intrusions. The soils of Britain are, on the whole, regarded as damp, but local areas vary in the amount of moisture as well as in their chemical composition, dissolved mineral content and oxygen. Soils may also vary in texture and colour. Each of these aspects has an effect on an artefact but none more so than a high moisture and oxygen content. In environments where oxygen is low (such as waterlogged conditions or damp clay), the survival of organic material is greatly improved. A dry or desiccated environment where there is little moisture, such as some caves, also favours preservation.

There is no universal system of soil classification but they can be broadly classified by the size of particles they contain and described using terms such as 'gravel', 'sand', 'silt' and 'clay' (see Table 1). To gain some idea of the particle size you can rub soil between fingers and thumb to judge the grittiness of a sandy soil, or the silky stickiness of clay.

Gravels

The survival of artefacts in gravels depends on the acidity and the permeability of the soil. Some waterlogged peaty gravels or alluvial mud can stain objects a dark brown.

Chalk

Artefacts made of organic material will not survive well in chalk soils and may be fragile, although stronger organic materials such as bone may be better preserved. Chalk residue can take a lot of effort to remove and some artefacts will still retain a white sheen long after they are dry and can deposit a white dust for some time afterwards. Avoid trying to vigorously wash off the chalk dust as this will only damage the artefact. Generally chalk is soft but it can also be consolidated, which means it may have to be scraped from an artefact. Do so with care.

Clay

Clay absorbs and holds large amounts of water. The particles are too small to be felt with the fingers or to be seen. When pressed between the fingers it leaves a smear. Often acidic it can contribute to the corrosion of many metal artefacts, but organics can be preserved well.

Sand

Sands allow easy drainage and highly sandy soil will not hold much water. The grains are clearly visible and can be felt with the fingers. If squeezed together in the hand, sandy soils will fall apart when released. They vary considerably in acidity and so artefacts will have variable survival. Very dry sand, such as that found in deserts, has beautifully preserved a wide range of artefacts, such as the mummies and other treasures of Egypt.

Decay of artefacts

The rate of decay of an artefact depends on the material it is constructed from and the environment in which it is buried. Some mineral inclusions found in soil can aid preservation, such as copper which can help conserve organics – wood, leather and textiles have been found in prehistoric copper mines in central southeast Europe. Similarly, highly salty soil will preserve some organic items, just as it has been used to preserve food for thousands of years. The salt mines from Iron Age Hallstatt, Austria, have yielded well-preserved organic remains. Bone, wood and

Examples with approx pH values	pH	Relative Strength
NaOH Solution (14.0)	— 14	x10000000
	— 13	x1000000
Household Bleach (12.5)	— 12	x100000
Household Ammonia (11.6)	— 11	x10000
Milk of Magnesia (9.9)	— 10	x1000
	— 9	x100
Baking Soda (8.4)		
Egg White/Sea Water (8.0)	— 8	x10
Pure Water (7.0)	— 7	x1
Cows Milk (6.4)	— 6	x10
Beef (5.5)		
Black Coffee (5.0)	— 5	x100
Apple Juice (4.0)	— 4	x1000
Cola/Vinegar (2.9)	— 3	x10000
Lemon Juice (2.3)	— 2	x100000
Limes (1.9)		
	— 1	x1000000
Hydrochloric Acid (0.1)	— 0	x10000000

TABLE 2 SOME pH VALUES

shell survive well in alkaline or neutral soils, but are destroyed in acidic soils often within a few years of deposition. Glass will decay in alkaline soils. Acid soils preserve pollen and other plant materials.

An object that has existed in a sealed soil environment for some time will reach a point of stasis where decomposition will be reduced to a slow and steady rate. Only when conditions change, such as exposure to air when excavated, is corrosion accelerated. Temperate climates are not generally good for organics with their fluctuating temperatures and high humidity, but in some highly acidic conditions various organics may survive. In acid bogs the oxidisation of metals is largely prevented and so a good recovery is possible. Bodies removed from bogs often lack the bones but the skin is almost perfectly preserved – tanned into leather.

pH

The mixture of chemicals in soils makes them either acidic or alkaline. The acidity and alkalinity of materials, including soils, are measured on a pH scale which runs from 0 (very acidic) to 14 (very alkaline or 'basic') with 7 being neutral.

pH or the 'potential of hydrogen' is the concentration of hydrogen ions in a solution. The more hydrogen ions present, the stronger the acid effect. pH is a logarithmic scale with each whole value representing a ten-fold increase or decrease in the acidity therefore the most acidic substances (pH of 0) are 10 million times as acidic as water. However, it is rare to find soils at the ends of the pH range.

As plants and micro-organisms can be responsible for the natural relocation of objects, the pH of a soil can indicate the kind of living organisms, and therefore the kind of movement, that can be expected. Most plants and micro-fauna (such as spiders, beetles, grubs, mites, slugs, snails and woodlice) prefer soils starting at a pH of 4 and reaching an alkalinity of 10. Lower than 4pH and nutrients cannot dissolve and be available to plants (and to the animals that eat the plants). Healthy plants also need bacteria to break down decayed matter and most bacteria prefer a pH of around 6.3-6.8 (although fungus, molds and anaerobic bacteria have a broader tolerance). There are plants which prefer more acidic soils such as azaleas and rhododendrons which grow well in a soil of 4.5-5.5 pH. The pH of most soils will not be static but vary according to different temperatures, rainfall or plant growth.

The pH in soils can be determined in a number of ways:

1. *Observation of predominent flora* – most plants prefer neutral or alkaline soil, so if the few that prefer reasonably acidic soils are present in quantity it is likely the pH is between 7-4.5. Acid-loving plants include birch, foxgloves, heathers, rhododendrons, azaleas, gorses, Scots Pine, strawberries and potatoes.
2. *Using a pH testing kit* – a sample of soil is mixed with water and barium sulphate powder. The water changes colour and is compared to a standard set of colours to measure the pH.
3. *Using an electronic pH meter* – a rod inserted into the soil is used to record the concentration of hydrogen ions.

The pH of any given soil is not constant and may vary according to rainfall, temperature, plant and animal life – even on a daily basis. The levels of pH an artefact is subjected to can be a significant factor in its survival.

TABLE 3 ARTEFACT SURVIVAL

ALKALINE SOILS		NEUTRAL SOILS		ACIDIC SOILS	
Survival possible	*Survival unlikely*	*Survival possible*	*Survival unlikely*	*Survival possible*	*Survival unlikely*
Alabaster	Glass	Bone	Alabaster	Amber	Alabaster
Bone	Horn	Ceramics	Horn	Ceramics	Bone
Copper	Leather	Copper	Leather	Earthenware	Ceramics
Earthenware	Shale	Glass	Limestone	Gold	Copper
Gold	Textiles	Gold	Textile	Jet	Earthenware's
Lead	Tin	Iron	Tin	Porcelain	Horn
Limestone	Wood	Lead	Wood	Roman glass	Iron
Porcelain	Zinc	Shale	Zinc	Shale	Lead
Silver		Silver		Silver	Leather
Slag		Slag		Slag	Limestone
Stoneware				Stoneware	Medieval glass
Terracotta					Textiles
					Tin
					Wood
					Zinc

DEPOSITIONS

An object in the archaeological record is there either due to primary deposition, or secondary deposition.

Primary deposition
This describes objects which enter the archaeological record and have not moved until excavation. This is known as the 'Pompeii Premise' where everything was believed to be excavated in its original position from when the volcanic eruption struck. Primary deposition is relatively rare as an area is inhabited by humans is generally popular with later generations who will disturb items as they re-use the ground.

Secondary deposition
These are items that have moved from their original position either by natural or cultural transforms (see below).

NATURAL AND CULTURAL TRANSFORMS

Michael Schiffer developed a theory of deposition that describes the formation and development of the archaeological record. He coined the phrases 'N' and 'C', referring to 'natural' and 'cultural' transforms. The natural formation processes refer to environmental events whilst the cultural formation processes include the deliberate or accidental activities of humans. On any given site either or both of these processes can act together to result in the appearance of the site when excavated.

Natural or 'N' Transforms

Soil layers are not naturally static, but are subject to continuous changes. Most often these changes are small on a daily basis but build slowly over centuries to completely alter the structure of the layers. Some natural changes can be faster and more dramatic – such as earthquakes or landslips.

These changes come about through a variety of means – mechanical changes can impact all landscapes: frost, ice and drought will all break up the soil; wind can either create or fill in ground depressions; and rain may wash materials from one area to another. Soil can roll down hills and build up when it reaches a barrier such as hedges or trees. Strong winds can uproot plants. Rivers erode their banks and can deposit the material far away. The sea is capable of undermining huge cliffs and carrying the soil to create beaches and mudflats.

Other changes come about from the action of plant roots pushing apart the soil and moving objects it contains. The extent of the root system will reach to a comparable volume to the canopy of a plant, but spread more laterally – it is a common misconception that the root system of trees mirrors the branches above, but they are actually quite shallow and tend to reach depths of less than 2m (however, the tap roots of large trees such as oak and beech can go much deeper).

Even a small sample of soil will include thousands of bacteria and animals living in water-filled pores, air gaps and burrows. Micro-organisms, such as bacteria, will break up buried organic debris, shifting the soil where the debris had been. The soil is in constant turmoil, ants and other invertebrates will move large amounts in their nest-making, bringing soil to the surface where it can cover an item or feature. Larger animals like rabbits and badgers will make burrows – pushing material up, down and sideways. Archaeologists will often turn over mole hills to see if anything has been brought up from lower levels – prehistoric flint work can often by found in this way.

All of these changes affect the makeup of the soil. Chemicals and minerals fluctuate, if an area is leeched out by rainfall it may be replaced with completely different materials. Industrialisation and acid rain can affect areas hundreds of miles away. Other aspects of the soil, such as colour and texture, can change so much that the current soil of any given location may bear little resemblance to the soils that were there in the past.

The organism probably most active in the displacement of soil layers is the earthworm. Earthworms are found all over the world and can reach lengths of 1.5m, but most European species are about 15-25cm. They usually live at the ground level and in topsoil to a depth of around 20-30cm but will burrow deeper in cold or dry conditions. Some will burrow up to depths of 2m, stopping only when they encounter a hard surface. Earthworms prefer alkaline or neutral soils and occur rarely in soils of less than 4.5 pH. They favour areas that have avoided cultivation and in optimum locations a worm population can reach half a million per acre. The activities of worms are important when one understands that the amount of soil moved from lower levels to the surface ranges from 2-24 tons per acre per annum with British earthworms (37 tons on the Continent) (Atkinson, 221), although this varies according to the species present and the size of the local population. As the worms move the earth upwards the cavities created by the many tunnels and burrows fall in so that, although the ground level remains constant to the eye, it is actually continually changing. An experiment to illustrate this would be to place an object such as a coin on a lawn or ground surface and leave it. Within a few years it will be subsumed and be found some distance under the surface. According to Darwin, who was the first to study worm activity in 1837, the rate of vertical displacement of an object is about 5cm in every ten years (Atkinson, 222). Worms will find their way through gaps in any hard surface such as tiles, cement or opus signium (Roman cement) gradually moving earth above them – the displacement is generally slow, accumulating to about 10cm in a century (Atkinson, 222). Atkinson concluded that:

Earthworm

...significant archaeological finds have been displaced downwards from the position in which they were originally deposited; and in some cases at least the amount of displacement may have been sufficient materially to alter the apparent Stratigraphic relationships of the objects concerned.

This is borne out in an example quoted in Barker (139) when eighteenth- and nineteenth-century sherds were found at Wroxeter on the surface of a Roman street – they had moved some 60cm–1m downwards.

Certain earthworms also take down small stones, shell fragments and seeds to line their burrows where they lie during dry weather. With each season the chambers fall in and leave a layer known to archaeologists as the 'pea grit' or 'split pea' level.

With all displacement mechanisms, an object will eventually reach a point where sinking is at a minimum and it will settle into equilibrium with its matrix.

Anthropogenic or 'C' Transforms

Natural processes can see the sinking of stones and artefacts but anthropogenic action can see it reversed with ploughing bringing up objects. This will usually be about 1m but as sites become multi-layered this can mean a displacement of 1m per layer (Goodyear, 27). Other anthropogenic action can produce multi-component sites formed after years of frequent depositing of debris, or debris being used as a rubble infill to produce a flat base for rebuilding. Most urban sites will have stratified sequences with a series of rebuilding. Other anthropogenic action includes wells cutting through several layers, or forestry where artefacts will be moved from the original location.

2

BASIC EQUIPMENT
AND ARRANGEMENTS

There are a number of items to obtain and arrangements to make when running an excavation that will improve the safety of working conditions and increase the effectiveness of finds processing.

ON SITE

High visibility jackets
Health and safety regulations state these must be available for use, and worn, on all sites where machinery is being operated.

Hard hat
A hard hat must be worn on all sites when a mechanical digger or machinery is being operated. Health and safety regulations state they must be available for use. Keep a note of the date of the hat and do not wear past the expiry date.

Site boots
Steel in-soled boots should be worn in keeping with health and safety regulations.

Leaf trowel

Trowel
The trowel used in British archaeology is the 10cm pointing trowel, the same type bricklayers and masons use. As processors are often called upon to excavate finds it is necessary to have one. Never use a cheap one as these are riveted rather than forged and have a tendency to come apart when being used. Standard trowels can also be used as a scale in photographs.

Leaf trowel
A leaf, or plaster trowel, is used by plasters for small areas. It is useful for fine excavating (see above).

WASHING THE FINDS

Water
On British sites water can be acquired in a number of ways. A lease can be obtained from the local water authority and a licence taken out for a number of gallons of water per day. With a lease of this kind a standpipe will be supplied or, if the site is near a water hydrant, a key and bar will be issued. Some water companies sell keys with the licence that can be retained by the unit and can be used throughout the water company's area.

Once a standpipe is installed a hose can be attached which, with enough pressure, can provide a strong flow of water to clean the finds.

Another way to get water on site is to hire water bowsers. Although each bowser contains approx 950 litres they constantly need topping up, adding to costs. In addition, as well as the cost of hire there is usually an extra charge for the power hose, so it is worth phoning around and getting a variety of quotes.

If a mains water source is available, sinks can be included, and small finds processed (volunteers come in useful here) at the same time as large context finds outside.

Drums/tanks

Impromptu processing areas can often be constructed cheaply and quickly. A converted oil drum or a metal tank, with an overflow pipe, can quickly be made. Place a large wire basket onto the drum or tank. Line the basket with a fine plastic mesh of approximately 200-250 microns to protect small items from falling through. This mesh can be obtained from many museum supply companies. If using bowsers, drums or tanks drainage channels or an area for free-flowing water need to be made away from any excavations.

Electricity

External electricity supplies can be arranged through the local electricity supplier.

Power sprays

Power sprays running on mains electricity, or a petrol/diesel generator, are commercially available and can be invaluable, often cutting processing time by two thirds. The less powerful spray the longer the cleaning time whilst high-power hoses will clean rapidly and usually quite thoroughly. Another advantage of a power spray is that the strength of the spray can be adjusted with much more accuracy than with nozzle sprays on a hose. A gentle spray can be used for the smaller or more delicate items and the powerful one can be used for bulk finds.

For a site with a collection of artefacts that requires at least 2-5 hours a day washing, an industrial machine such as a Kercher should be considered. These provide pressures in excess of 100 bar, much greater than that of the small domestic sprays on offer through chains such as B&Q. The difference in cost is quite large however, with the smaller domestic machines retailing for £50 upwards, whilst the industrial ones range from £400–£1,000.

The Kercher and like machines usually come with a hose of 10m but some come with 15m. If necessary a connector and more hose length should be purchased in case the machine is a fair distance from the water supply.

Although power sprays can be invaluable they also need to be carefully stored and maintained, which can be difficult if storage space and security is at a premium.

Water hose
The longer the better. Where a standing pipe is available a general garden hose with spray nozzles can be used. Hoses and a variety of fittings can be cheaply purchased in any garden shop or nursery.

Hose adaptors
Have three: one to attach to a tap; one if a hose extension is needed; and a spare.

Adjustable spray heads
These should be adjustable from spray to single stream. Have two, one to keep as a spare.

Industrial insulating tape
Useful for many jobs but particularly in case the hose does not fit the tap tightly, so must be waterproof.

Plastic washing-up bowls
For the processing of small finds. Several solid bowls will be needed; some of them meshed. (This can be done by cutting the base out of a bowl, fitting a variety of fine meshes as required, and using industrial insulating tape to fix.)

Plastic mesh
Plastic mesh which is needed in washing-up bowls or in cleaning tanks can be bought in a variety of gauges but the most useful is 200-250 micron which will secure small items without them being too minute. It comes on rolls and is sold in lengths.

Plastic plant spray
These sprays can be bought at many high street shops, garden centres and nurseries and can be used for wetting small finds. Spraying mosaics will often highlight the colours and hard-to-see context lines can be made more visible when wet. Do not be tempted to re-use window

spray or other bottles from home as they will have residues of chemicals which may react with the objects being cleaned.

Waterproof coat, trousers/wellingtons or waterproof boots

Vital to keep the processor dry and clean, although in hot weather they can become uncomfortable to wear. Try to avoid cheap waterproofs as they tend not to have air holes for the release of moisture, nor do most of them have the internal layer designed to keep the wearer cool.

Gloves

Thermal woollen gloves are widely available at a reasonable price and are worn under surgical gloves to protect the processors hands from the cold.

Surgical gloves can be used on their own or over thermal gloves. The combination of the two is effective in cutting down wastage as fewer gloves are disposed of. Surgical gloves will protect from infections and rusting staples. Do not use petrol station gloves, these are too flimsy. In spite of their usefulness surgical gloves become very slippery when wet and tear easily, so some processors do not use them. Washing-up gloves are another option, but these can be too thick, especially when carrying out delicate work, such as finger washing on leather. The choice of gloves comes down, in the main, to personal preference.

Always make sure gloves fit as if they are too large it will be difficult to lift and feel with them.

Goggles

Health and safety regulations state they must be available for use.

Masks

Masks should be worn when dealing with lead and excess mould, but are often bulky and become hot. Although most people prefer not to use masks, in some situations Health and Safety may insist on their being worn, so they must be made readily available.

Earplugs

Disposable earplugs will often be necessary if working with mechanical machinery. Alternatively ear mufflers which attach to a hard hat can be used and although more bulky they are more effective than earplugs.

A selection of brushes

Buckets

Buckets are always needed if water has to be carried to the processing area, but also for carrying finds, moving rubbish and a variety of uses.

Nail brushes/toothbrushes/scrubbing brushes

Buy new brushes rather than bring ones in from home, as these may have toothpaste or cleaning chemical residue. Do not buy brushes with hard bristles as they will damage finds. Have a range of brushes available, for example a nail brush to use on hard surfaces where possible damage is kept to a minimum, and a hand-brush for removing dirt during excavation so that outlines of the context can be seen.

Sponges

These can be bought from many high street shops. Do not introduce soap into them as can take a long time to clean through and the chemicals in the soap could be detrimental to the material being cleaned.

Wire

Pieces of fine wire are useful for cleaning the interior of pipe stems or turned glass rims. Use coated wire to avoid scratching objects.

Probes

All pointed metal objects must be used with care for personal safety and the protection of the finds. Pressure should not be applied when using metal probes. Never use metal tools on any organic artefact recovered from a waterlogged site.

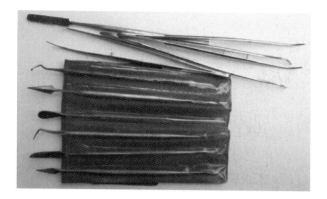

Probes

Dental tools or wax-carving tools – dental tools can usually be scrounged from a dentist who no longer requires them. Wax-carving tools can be bought cheaply in art shops.

Needles can be used for very fine work, but all pointed metal objects must be used with care.

Penknife – the Swiss army types have a number of useful points.

Wooden drinks stirrer – for cleaning artefacts wet and dry. They are particularly useful for angling into nooks and crannies. Most can be scrounged from coffee shops or restaurants.

Wooden tongue depressors – can be used for trowelling and can be whittled to required shapes.

Toothpicks/matchsticks are useful as they are often softer than the material they are being used to clean. A range of spoons are useful for the removal of dirt and for excavating post holes.

Magnet
To test for iron when corrosion levels may mask the material or to see if there is a significant amount of iron left within a rust corrosion level. Only a small, portable one is needed.

Masking tape
Masking tape is essential for all sorts of jobs and is easy to use (try finding the end of Sellotape with wet surgical gloves on!). It does not mark like Sellotape and can be removed easily, often without any damage to the surface. Masking tape can also be used for temporary holding of objects such as pottery for short-term displays.

Stanley knife
Or any kind of stout cutting knife with replaceable blades, although avoid cheap ones as the blades will snap and become dull much quicker.

Large plastic sheets
Can be used to wrap large objects, either to shield them or keep them damp. Avoid the thin plastic sheeting designed to cover furniture when decorating; instead use something that will last.

Pens
A waterproof pen is a must, in case labels have to be re-written. Berol Permanent Marker, Autoseal Ink, Staedtler or Artline brands have proved to be effective.

Tweezers
For removal of fine particles or for lifting small items such as beads.

Cotton buds
Ideal for getting into those difficult nooks and crannies, but buy natural cotton not cheap substitutes.

Magnifying glass/hand lens
A good-quality magnifying glass is essential for examining details too fine for the naked eye, and identifying difficult materials such as bone and ivory. A 10x lens is ideal for most situations.

Ranging rod
For photographing finds in situ.

Measuring tape
Measuring finds in situ as well as multiple other tasks. A retractable 3m or 5m with plastic tape is usual.

First Aid kit
There is no mandatory list of contents for first aid boxes. Deciding what to include depends on the employer's assessment of first aid needs. The Health and Safety Executive provides information and advice.

Notices
Health and safety sheets on anthrax, lead poisoning, Weil's disease, manual lifting, tetanus and dealing with human remains.

Distilled water
Available from local suppliers and used for the cleaning of fragile finds and for washing finds where local water is not suitable (it may contain salt for instance).

DRYING THE FINDS

Bread crates
These are invaluable as they are sturdy, can carry a lot, have handles that fold down and can be packed easily.

Plastic mushroom crates
Most of these can be scrounged from fruit/vegetable vendors. They are extremely useful for carrying large assemblages or finds and can be stacked free-standing saving shelf space.

Seed trays
Black plastic oblong trays used for seeding plants are cheaply available from gardening shops or nurseries. Long-lasting, easily transported and stackable they are ideal for drying finds. Always remember to buy uniform sizes or stacking will be difficult. Try to avoid buying cheap versions as they have a tendency to bend easily when under pressure.

Newspaper
Collect newspapers from diggers, etc to put finds on to dry (for more details see page 64)

CLEANING DRY FINDS

Brushes
Use paint brushes for removing loose dirt from fragile items and for brushing dust away from display tables. Buy good-quality brushes with

natural hair as cheap brushes tend to shed their hairs over the finds and nylon bristles will dissolve if used with solvents. Soft bristles are best as no pressure should be applied to the object and sizes 2-5cm are good all round sizes. Bristles can be cut to whatever size or shape is required. Photographic 'puffer' brushes are useful for blowing away loose dirt. Brushes can be cleaned with water or acetone but take care with acetone as sometimes the paint on the handle will come away and flakes of paint may get caught up with artefacts.

Plastic food storage boxes

Plastic food storage boxes are available in varying sizes with snap-on lids, and are vital for storing fragile finds, metal finds (in association with silica gel), and waterlogged finds.

Vacuum cleaner

To remove loose dirt a low powered hand-held vacuum cleaner can be used; these are available from many high street electrical stores. Place a piece of gauze or muslin over the mouth to make the suction less forceful, and to avoid small items being sucked up.

IN THE FINDS CABIN

It is essential for the finds processor to have access to a portacabin. A dedicated cabin for finds is advisable but if this is not possible then a significant space from another cabin will be needed. Whether the cabin is dedicated or shared, the main consideration is secure storage and the facility to allow finds to dry in a heated area without being disturbed by other people who may be using the same area. In the event of valuable finds being recovered, arrangements need to be put into place as to where they will be taken at the end of each day to ensure their safety.

The heating in a cabin is often of a temperature comfortable for the people working in it which may not necessarily suit the needs of the artefacts being dried and if this is the case then an alternative drying area must be arranged. The cabin should also have adequate ventilation as the use of a heater without ventilation will encourage the growth of mould and fungus. This could cause breathing difficulties and other problems for people working in the cabin.

Shelving

If a dedicated finds cabin is available it should be large enough to allow shelving (long enough to allow for storing the seed trays) to be erected alongside as many walls as possible. This will avoid having to store trays on the floor where the heat will not reach them as effectively as higher up. Shelves can either be the purpose-built sort or the self-build kit type.

Sinks

A double sink is preferable: one for cleaning and one for rinsing. Spray heads can be attached to the tap. Most dirt should be scraped from the objects first, as using a sink will mean an accumulation of dirt in the water so a filter on the plug-hole should be fitted or the dirt will block the drains.

Heating

Heating is a must, particularly during the autumn and winter months. The finds need to dry at a consistent temperature, so the cabin must have at least one power point dedicated for a heater, preferably a radiator as they provide a steady heat. Try and avoid fluctuations in the heating as this may cause the finds to dry out too quickly and lead to damage. The heating should be used throughout the day but switched off at night.

Tables/chairs

Tables should be large enough to use for sorting through the finds as well as undertaking documentation. A chair or two will also be needed. Often sites will have pubic open days so spare trestle tables to display the finds are useful.

RECORDING/ILLUSTRATING FINDS

Angle-poise lamp/spare bulbs

When working closely with finds, such as during illustration, it is better to have a strong, local light.

Mapping pen and nibs

Recording sheets/cards
A good supply of the unit's standardised recording sheets should be available, consisting of bulk cataloguing sheets, accession cards and context labels.

Pens
Use a long lasting, waterproof pen (see pages 56 and 74) such as the Berol Permanent Marker, the Autoseal Ink or those made by Staedler or Artline for use on the context labels. Always use black as this is the easiest colour to read and will photocopy well.

Mapping pens and nibs
Mapping pens consist of changeable steel nibs with a wooden or ceramic handle and are used for the marking finds. The nibs wear out quickly so it is best to order a dozen or so nibs. These pens take a little getting used to as if pressed too hard the nibs will splay and become useless. There is an art to having enough ink in the nib without it dropping a blob when used. With new users, fingers can quickly become stained with ink so wet wipes can be handy.

Drawing pens
Drawing pens are needed to ensure drawings are permanent. The most popular are the Rotring Isograph or Faber-Castell TG range with nibs from 0.1-0.5mm. The nibs on these pens are very sensitive and if pressed hard will be damaged, making them difficult to use.

Black and white ink
Use good quality ink that is long-lasting. White ink is needed for marking on some pottery where black ink would not show up. Rotring or

Windsor & Newton inks have proven long-lasting. Note that these inks may dissolve when used with a Paraloid/varnish base.

Tippex or whitener
For stationery use only, never use on finds.

Pencils/ pencil sharpener
Use HB or a soft pencil as the writing can be seen more easily. Propeller pencils are useful as saves on sharpening but are more expensive.

Scalpel
A Swann Norton 10 is the most commonly used with handle number 3 as it will take a variety of blades, the most useful of which are numbers 10 and 15. These can be bought from any art shop.

Eraser
Do not buy a cheap rubber as these tend to be very hard and can tear the paper. Buy a good quality one such as those made by Staedtler. A useful eraser is a putty rubber which will crumble if used too hard, but can be used to remove all sorts of marks from a variety of surfaces.

Ruler
A plastic ruler for measuring and drawing.

Stapler and staples
For paperwork and stapling the finds bags. Avoid small and cheap versions as they will not last.

Callipers
These are advisable for the correct measuring of artefacts that are difficult to draw flat. Always use plastic, never metal and those with a small measuring wheel which give accurate recordings to a millimetre.

Soldering wire/French curve
For using against artefacts as a representation of the shape or form.

Pair of compasses
For drawing circles when illustrating, and for drawing a radius chart.

Lever arch files
For the storage of the bulk catalogue sheets and other miscellaneous paperwork.

Paraloid B72
Available from conservation/paint suppliers for marking up and cleaning brushes.

Acetone
Used for surface preparation when marking up and for cleaning pens and brushes.

Artefact thesaurus
Descriptions of items should be made according to the thesaurus recommended by the museum where the finds are destined. There are a number of thesauruses, including the British Museum, England Heritage, Museum of London. Use only the names that are listed in the thesaurus.

PACKING FINDS

Context labels
A minimum of two labels must be included in each bagged item, so an adequate supply is needed.

Bags
Do not use self-sealing bags; these may spill finds as the self-sealing fails over time. Use plastic bags of varying size, e.g. 15.25cm x 22.9cm; 20cm x 30.5cm; 30.5cm x 45.7cm; and 45.7cm x 61cm (see 59 and 70).

Acid-free tissue paper
For wrapping delicate finds.

Acid-free polyethylene foam
Needed to protect packed finds.

Black waterproof markers
For marking boxes, leaving notices for diggers and various other uses.

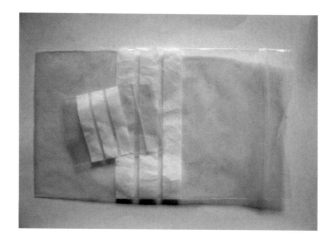

Self-sealing bags

Bubble wrap
For protecting finds particularly during moving. It is a protective cush-
ioning material made from low-density polyethylene. The rolls come in
several widths and various bubble sizes, though 9mm bubble size is most
widely used for artefacts.

Boxes to store processed finds
Acid-free 'shoe' boxes are recommended for small finds as these can be
stacked and carried easily.

Silica gel
For use with the plastic food storage boxes when storing metals, particularly iron (see page 73).

Box labels
Self-adhesive standardised labels to identify contents. Two kinds, accession labels and bulk labels.

Crystal boxes
Some finds might be valuable or fragile and need to be placed in protective boxes. Clear polystyrene boxes for delicate and valuable finds,
sometimes called crystal boxes, come in a variety of sizes and have a
secure lid.

Cotton gloves
Hands will always carry a residue of grease, salts and acids. Cotton gloves will protect objects during handling but they can be slippery when handling smooth surfaces. Varieties with 'pimples' to give a better grip are available.

Heat sealer
For sealing bags containing finds that need to be suspended in water (see page 71).

CONSERVATION

Bandages
For those fragile finds recovered in situ which need reinforcement or support before removal.

Plaster of Paris
Also used for fragile finds which need support before removing. It is cheap, simple to apply and easy to remove in the lab.

Aluminium foil
Can be used as a separator between an artefact and the plaster of Paris.

MISCELLANEOUS

X-ray
If there is a collection of metals then thought can be given to finding an x-ray facility to identify iron items. On heavily encrusted pieces, details may be obscured and x-ray will reveal the make-up of the piece, and details of the technology used in manufacturing. For example, a feature of some swords, particularly Damask swords, is their unique method of folding, twisting and forging which can be seen in x-rays. Recording an item in x-ray will also provide information as to whether the piece is worth conserving.

Precious metals need to be registered with the coroner's office so the contact number for the local office should be to hand.

3

EXCAVATION

COLLECTION POLICY

Either before or during excavation, a collection, or sampling, policy is usually established. If large amounts of a single material such as building material, pottery or shell are being recovered it may be necessary to retain only those pieces which include diagnostic information (such as pot rims or decorations). This strategy saves on time, money and resources, and sampling can provide an efficient indication of the nature of the assemblage. Although this collection policy is commonplace, some finds specialists disagree. One of their concerns is that most sites will have a number of inexperienced diggers who lack the ability to recognise what is actually diagnostic; the collection will therefore be skewed.

Take for example the collection of Roman building material. A roof comprising of tegula and imbrix will usually exist in the ratio of 2:1 tegula to imbrix. If this ratio is compromised due to an inefficient collection policy, it may make it difficult to establish the exact nature of the structure. Another consideration is that the temper, or fabric, of building material and pottery can be very varied, and without resource to a microscope and/ or expert knowledge it may be impossible to recognise various tempers in the field. At this time there are large gaps in the catalogue of tempers of

Roman building materials that need to be filled. Finally, a further criticism voiced by some specialists is that often they are not included in initial policy decisions, the policy being decided by the site management. With so few excavation reports being published it can be difficult to know what finds are being recovered in a general area and what to look out for. Specialists can help to fill these gaps by providing information which may not be generally available to the units involved.

General collection policies
General collection policies exist, unless superseded by site specific policies. Here are some standard guidelines:

Do not collect:
- unstratified bone
- non-artefact wood
- unstratified building material, mortar, plain wall plaster, post medieval bricks
- shell of any kind (unless it is an obvious artefact and shows signs of deliberate modification such as having a hole punched in it (see page 118)) as in order for shell information to be of any use a large sample needs to be collected. This will be decided by the site managers.

EXCAVATING POTTERY

The recovery of pottery is a primary objective on most sites as these are the finds that most often provide a secure source of dating and need a note on the excavation of pottery.

Pottery forms changed quickly so a chronological sequence has been developed for most pottery types. The excavation of pottery however, like most finds, is dominated by what is most visible. Certain pottery types are recovered more often than others, such as Samian ware, the bright shiny Roman pottery that stands out against the dark earth. On the other hand coarsewares blend in with the dark earth and have, in comparison, a lower recovery rate. Their relative invisibility also renders them liable to be hit with a mattock/pickaxe.

On the whole pottery survives well in most soil conditions. Certain pottery however will require care when excavating. Throughout the pre-

Dark pottery against a dark background (left) is often hard to see compared to brightly coloured pottery (right)

historic periods, and later during the Anglo-Saxon periods just after the Roman departure, some pottery was made in low firing conditions, such as bonfires. When this happens the outside of the pottery is hardened but the inside remains relatively soft. This can easily be seen by the banding of colours in a broken sherd. Low-fired pottery will disintegrate in circumstances where there is a high moisture content so when excavating, particularly in the rain, do not leave it in the tray to become wet. Place it in a polythene bag or cover the tray.

All fragments of pottery from within a secure context should be collected as they may be from broken pots which may be possible to reconstruct. Detailed chronological sequences exist for most pottery forms of the Roman, Saxon, medieval and post-medieval periods, however gaps do exist and fragments from unstratified contexts can contribute in chronological sequencing. Therefore collect unstratified pottery only if it is diagnostically important as these may help to extend knowledge of particular categories, new variants, more complete examples or other new details.

Do not bother separating pottery into colours or types (unless of course specifically asked to do so); as the pottery specialist will do any necessary separations. However, if unusual items occur it may be worth bringing them to the finds supervisor's attention. Note that some processors may be volunteers and may lack experience in recognising those items that require special treatment such as burnished pottery. Pottery from the Neolithic times onwards could be subjected to burnishing. This method took place when the pot was still in its leathery state before firing and the outside rubbed with hard objects such as bones, wood or stones. After firing the exterior would have a shiny look. The purpose of burnishing was to close the pores of the clay as much as possible to make it waterproof. It can be seen on Neolithic pottery and Roman black burnished ware particularly when it begins to flake away. If it is felt that an item does need attention then bag separately and write an explanatory note, such as 'burnished pottery', in the description area of the context label.

Whole pots

Complete pots are fairly rare and where they are found they tend to be recovered as grave goods, as vessels for cremation, or from wells, abandoned kilns, or hoards. If excavating a whole or partial vessel of any kind do not remove any earth from inside the pot – particularly if it has been recovered from a grave context, as it may contain remains of food offerings. The remains will need to be sieved by the processor in case it contains inclusions which can give an indication of what the vessel was used for and the plants of the time. On Plantation House, a Roman site excavated by MoLAS (Museum of London Archaeological Services), a crucible was recovered with a conglomeration in the base. When this was removed and examined it was found to be paint and was later matched to some painted wall plaster that was recovered from the same site. Had the contents been removed on-site, this information would have been lost.

RECOVERY METHODS

Care should be taken over the recovery of finds regardless of their condition and/or perceived value. A single sherd may seem unimportant but, as stated above, it may be of type not currently catalogued.

When a context reveals an accumulation of artefacts, this may indicate that manufacturing activities have taken place (such as hammer scale or moils), and should be brought to the site manager's attention.

Experienced diggers are said to have an 'eye' for finds. Getting your 'eye in' is purely a case of practice and experience and cannot be taught. Even so, experienced diggers may have difficulty when faced with unfamiliar pot in unfamiliar types of soil. The best tip is to look for shapes and lines. Straight lines, squares or triangles are not readily found in nature, and it is this, more than colour, which can be the giveaway to a good find.

When finds are recovered they may often be deformed due to the weight of the soil. This is particularly true of soft materials such as lead and copper. Each artefact has its own history, its condition and how it came to be in that condition, and if the piece is recovered in a twisted or deformed shape no attempt should be made to alter its history by trying to restore it to an original shape. In addition, if an item is distorted it may be weak and any attempt to manipulate it may damage it further.

Never use a trowel or hard tool to clean off surface dirt; if it does need cleaning, use fingers, brushes or sponges so that the items will not get marked. Do as little cleaning as possible in the field, do not empty the internal bases of pots or vessels as these may have remains in them which will need to be preserved. Some items may have shreds of textiles adhering to them and if cleaned roughly this information may be lost.

TROWELLING

Finds must be removed by stratigraphic layer. They should never be dug, pulled or levered out no matter how tempting it may be. If the neck of a pot is exposed whilst trowelling back a layer, it must remain in situ until the entire layer is reduced and the whole pot exposed, even if this takes days or months. Removing the find arbitrarily would not only put it at risk of being broken but valuable contextual information may be lost, particularly if the find is incorporated in other yet unseen layers. Although the piece itself may be easily seen other items may be obscured, so by excavating fully around all the items it will be easier to see the relationships between them. If an item is forced out too early this information may be lost. Understanding the find's relationship to those layers could be compromised. (When an artefact is recovered from two or more layers it is usual to assign it to the upper layer due to the tendency for items to sink (see Chapter 2)). An artefact must not be dug out individually, except when there is sound reason to do so, for example, if it is in need of immediate attention, or if by leaving the find overnight it would be in danger of theft or damage. In addition, it is not until the whole of the piece is cleared that it can be seen if it requires any conservation.

When it is appropriate to remove the find, clear the area around it as much as possible, particularly underneath, so that it will lift easily without force. If there is resistance continuing clearing until it is loose. It may be easier to pick at the soil with the point of the trowel rather than scraping, but do not touch the artefact directly as it may be scratched. If necessary leave a thin layer of earth which can be brushed away or removed with smaller tools such as a leaf trowel or dental picks. Do not lever the piece as this may create stresses and could result in it breaking. Never lift by handles or any other projections as these may be weak and may not support the rest of the piece.

If a find is to be left in situ overnight or for the weekend, it should be covered with a waterproof covering to protect it from the elements. If it is to be left for long periods then more stable arrangements need to be made such as re-covering the area with removed spoil so that the find remains as close to its original matrix as possible.

Keep alert for staining in the soil, such as green which may have been stained by copper remains, red for where iron may have been, or black for burning.

SHADOW FINDS

Finds do not always exist in solid, removable forms. Some may leave only a trace of their presence. The wood from the Wetwang chariot burials had decayed but the soil was so tightly packed it left cavities, which could be cast in a similar way to the bodies at Pompeii.

Perhaps the most quoted example of this kind is the Sutton Hoo ship excavation. The Sutton Hoo had became a ghost ship, for all the organic parts, including the corpse (if there had been one), had disappeared in the acidic sands. However, the sand had hardened and provided an almost exact mould of the ship's timbers. Most of the iron rivets had also disappeared leaving rows of red oxide stains, and over 1,500 rivets were recorded in this way. The site director C.W. Phillips in his 1940 account describes the find:

> the timbers of the ship had rotted away almost without exception, but since all but the burial chamber area had been filled in directly with sand while the ship was still whole none of the clench nails which held the ship together could move from their place even when the wood which they secured had disappeared. By careful work from the inside it was possible to remove all the content of the boat without displacing any of the nails which remained in their places on the sides of the excavation. This

process was aided by a change in the consistency of the sand which was to be found where the boat's timbers had once been. A dusty blackish layer, accompanied by some leached sand, could be felt for carefully by slowly shaving down the sand, and warning was given of its approach by the appearance of the bright red patches signalling the near presence of clench nails. In this way all the boat which survived was emptied so that the face of the excavation everywhere was the sand which had pressed against the timbers of the boat from the outside, and which sometimes still bore in recognisable form the imprint of the grain of wood. The only parts missing were the point of the bow and the end of the stern, the latter having been removed by the plough.

A record should be taken of the exact layout of staining in case the original form can be deduced. If the remains of shadow artefacts are considered to be of enough importance to retain, then the staining should be block removed, although it can sometimes be difficult to know where the stain ends, and the find can be truncated as a result (see page 51).

When dealing with objects which have disappeared leaving only a void, plaster of Paris can be poured in to form a mould of the shape. The most famous example of this is the moulds at Pompeii.

SIEVING

Wet and dry sieving is carried out for two reasons: to recover what would normally be missed by general excavation techniques; and to monitor what is being missed on any given site. Small items can be counted and compared to ordinary digging methods to see how under-represented they are. For these reasons sieved items should always be marked as being sieved.

Sieving can be more productive as small items such as coins, beads, gems, intaglio, and fragments of objects are generally more noticeable in a sieve than in the ground where they can blend in with the matrix. On a site worked by the author a large piece of Roman armour was recovered in an advanced state of decay. The surrounding matrix was a reddish colour (having absorbed the rust), when this was sieved several pieces of the armour, including a number of studs that held the plates together, were recovered. Had the area not been sieved it is probably much of this information would have been lost.

In Roman numismatics a series of small bronze coins from AD 307 onwards have been catalogued according to size in millimetres on the scale AE1 to AE4.

AE1 over 25mm

AE2 21mm–25mm

AE3 17mm–21mm

AE4 under 17mm

Roman AE coins

The smallest, the AE4, can be so small that some coins cannot hold all of the die design. Mostly they range from 13-17mm but smaller sizes are still common. (Obviously it may be difficult to know if a 17mm coin is an AE3 or an AE4 and those indistinguishable ones are referred to as AE3/4.) All the AE series are frequently found on sites and by metal detectors. The scale does not represent the value of the coin.

Sieving can be very time-consuming, so sampling strategies are often used. Other sites such as caves will often have all their deposits screened. Graves too are frequently sieved, particularly in the areas around the body, to ensure the recovery of small items such as beads or coins (some late Roman coins such as the AE4 (see box) can be very small at under 17mm, half the size of a British penny) (for more on graves see page 49). Before sieving starts there has to be some idea as to what sort of items are going to be recovered and therefore what mesh sizes and methods to use. However, fragments of less than 5mm are going to have limited typological use.

Wet sieves

Wet sieving has the advantage of washing the items at the same time and wet items are generally more visible. For bulk sieving, wire netting of different gauges can be obtained from many hardware shops. Using a truncated metal oil drum or some other firm frame, the wire can be securely bent around the ends. Over this a mesh of the desired size is attached to enable power spraying.

For smaller sieves many sites will make their own by purchasing rolls of mesh of 1mm for fine work and 4mm for bulk sieving, and a number of plastic washing-up bowls. The base of the bowl is cut away and the mesh stretched over the gap securing it with waterproof industrial tape. The sieves can either be used by pouring water through them, or by dipping in water and agitating. If wet sieving in sinks care must be taken with the drainage as the dissolved soil will accumulate and cause block-ages (see page 64).

DRY SIEVING

For quick on-site sieving a plastic hand-held domestic or garden sieve will suffice (do not use a metal one in case it damages the artefacts). However, on muddy sites, or when dealing with muddy items, these can quickly become clogged up. Dry sieves can also be made by converting plastic washing-up bowls as described in the section above.

For more refined work dedicated laboratory sieves can be purchased. These are a series of nested bronze sieves with graded mesh – the top sieve has the widest mesh, with each lower sieve progressively smaller. The stack is shaken so that the material moves through the top mesh down to the bottom. This way the larger pieces are left in the top sieve and a dust-like residue will be found in the base pan. Using these sieves can be time-consuming as their construction restricts the amount of material that can be placed in them at any one time, and so they are primarily used in laboratories to recover organic remains such seeds, grains and fish bones.

Recording sieved items
Finds recovered using sieving methods will not be closely stratified but all sieving should be taken from a specific context and therefore should be allocated that context number or, in the case of spits, a spit number. The label for the find should include sieving method information (see page 58) such as BS (bulk sieved), WS (wet sieved) or DS (dry sieved) and the mesh size. Catalogue sheets should include the same information.

METAL DETECTING

Metal detecting can be done by on-site staff or the Finds Processor, or members of the local metal-detecting clubs may be approached. The Finds Supervisor should have a list of local clubs who are willing to work on sites and usually they are more than happy to volunteer and donate their valuable experience.

WATERLOGGED CONDITIONS

Waterlogged conditions occur in a number of areas outside the obvious sea, river and lake deposits. They can be found in the remains of pits, wells, moats and ditches. Waterlogged deposits often preserve organics in far better quantity and condition than dry land, and the oxidisation of metals cannot occur. However, the chemical composition of some items may be changed.

On exposure to air some waterlogged items will begin to dry causing shrinkage and in some cases complete disintegration. Wood in particular will dry and shrink very quickly if allowed to do so (see page 129). Even as an individual piece is being excavated it may begin to dry out, so care should be taken to keep all relevant areas wet. A plastic houseplant spray can be used but ensure both the inside and the water is clean. If the artefact is going to be left overnight or longer, secure coverings need to be arranged which will keep the item wet.

The item should be allowed to dry out slowly under controlled circumstances.

Sites with a high salt content

A site near the sea will have specific problems with the high levels of salt in the air and artefacts left to dry in salt rich air may develop a very fine residue of crystals on which micro-organisms can feed. Items, particularly large ones that cannot be stored in the finds cabin should be kept covered as much as possible as salt will accelerate the corrosion process. If salt encrustation is evident remove to the processor as soon as possible (see page 67).

TABLE 4 ARTEFACT SURVIVAL

WATERLOGGED					
ALKALINE		NEUTRAL		ACIDIC	
Survival possible	*Survival unlikely*	*Survival possible*	*Survival unlikely*	*Survival possible*	*Survival unlikely*
Amber	Glass	Alabaster		Amber	Alabaster
Alabaster	Horn	Amber		Flax textiles	Bone
Bone	Silk textiles	Bone		Gold	Earthenware

WATERLOGGED					
ALKALINE		NEUTRAL		ACIDIC	
Survival possible	Survival unlikely	Survival possible	Survival unlikely	Survival possible	Survival unlikely
Ceramics	Tin	Ceramics		Hemp textiles	Flax textiles
Copper	Woollen textiles	Copper		Horn	Glass
Flax textiles	Zinc	Glass		Jet	Hemp textiles
Gold		Gold		Keratin	Lead
Hemp textiles		Horn		Leather	Limestone
Iron		Iron		Porcelain	Tin
Jet		Lead		Shale	Zinc
Lead		Leather		Silver	
Leather		Limestone		Slag	
Limestone		Shale		Stoneware	
Shale		Silver		Wood	
Slag		Slag			
Stoneware		Textiles			
Terracotta		Tin			
Wood		Zinc			

GRAVES

Grave goods are items placed in association with skeletal or cremated remains and all finds recovered from a grave must be recorded with direct association to the remains. The tradition of grave goods begins with the Neolithic, goes out of favour in the Iron Age, reappears with the Romans and continues throughout Anglo-Saxon times. Generally speaking, grave goods discontinue with Christianity (although it is a practice that has been revived in modern times with photographs or jewellery).

In addition to grave goods there are other finds such coffin nails (which will give an indication of the shape of the coffin), shroud pins, beads and small jewellery. In the feet areas of the skeleton look for nails which may be the only remains of hobnail shoes. It may be beneficial to use a metal detector to check the area first and sieve the entire grave to pick up small items unnoticed in the general excavation, such as small beads around the neck.

Some Roman shoes in particular were heavily nailed, which not only held the shoe together but also provided grip. Nailed shoes ended with the Romans and do not return until the nineteenth century.

Roman shoe

Examine the bones to see if there is any staining where objects may have been in contact with other materials: for example, copper will leave a green stain and iron a red. Make a note on the context label for the processor.

The soil will be also needed by the environmental processor. In particular look for stomach contents, parasites or flowers which may have been placed around the neck and more unusual items such as gall stones.

All grave finds must be left in situ until the skeleton is fully excavated and recorded. Photograph and/or draw all finds in situ so that a full analysis of the goods may be possible and a reconstruction of the grave made if necessary. Use vertical black and white photography, as opposed to oblique photography, as details will be easier to see.

WEATHER CONDITIONS

The weather can be detrimental to artefacts:

- A strong wind can generate dust that collects and abrade artefacts as they are washed – if processing outside erecting a screen for protection may help.
- Strong sunlight can bleach items, particularly organics, and also heat items too much and too quickly so as a general principle do not leave artefacts exposed.
- Frost can be detrimental particularly to large items such as statuary. The water inherent in a piece will expand as it freezes causing stress on the item. The resulting gaps can then fill with water and dust, leaving the item at risk.
- Rain may contain chemicals as a result of industrial pollution and so large items stored outside should be adequately protected.

UNSTRATIFIED FINDS (ALSO KNOWN AS STRAY FINDS)

If a find is recovered from spoil or other areas where the context is not secure, it should be regarded as unstratified. Unstratified finds are only worth keeping if they have intrinsic value. However, it can be difficult to assess this value given the lack of any meaningful context (see Collection Policy, page 39). Un-diagnostic body sherds of pottery and building material are not generally collected (see page 40). If a diagnostic but unstratified find is kept, a note should be made of its possible origins if the excavator has a good idea where it came from. Any soil or matrix still adhering to the item may give an indication of its original location.

BLOCK REMOVAL

If a find is too fragile to be removed it may be necessary to remove it as a block. Leave the find within its matrix and use a spade (this will give straighter lines than a shovel) to create a pedestal on, or in, which the find sits. Great care needs to be taken to ensure that the entire find is incorporated in the block, so that it is not severed upon removal. This can be done by excavating directly under the item and leaving two pedestals on each side to continue to provide support. Secure the find using bubble wrap, rubber sheeting, cling film or aluminium foil to prevent it moving and then secure the block on all sides with panels of plywood, hardboard or other rigid sheet material. Ensure the panels used will be strong enough to support the block. Before removal, the exact position of the block should be noted on the context sheet. Cut the block from the ground and slide a panel of metal or wood strong enough to hold the block underneath it and lift. Place in a box or crate large enough to take both the pedestal and the item leaving enough room around it to pack it with newspaper or bubble wrap, ensuring they are not in contact with the find.

Bandaging an item

If a piece is fragile such, as pot with many cracks which would give way upon lifting, bandaging may ensure it is removed without losing parts. Wrap the bandage around the item so that it is firm and secure but not so tight as to cause damage to the artefact. When using strips that cross over, start by wrapping the new strip nearly a complete circle over the previous strip, to provide as much stability as possible. Secure the end with masking tape or safety pins making absolutely sure that the pin in no way touches the artefact inside. It may be necessary to wrap the bandage around the object vertically as well as horizontally. With difficult protruding parts, buffer these first with acid-free tissue paper or bubble wrap before bandaging.

Using plaster of Paris

If a find is recovered that is not within a matrix but which is too fragile to remove, it may need to be coated in plaster of Paris or polyurethane foam to keep intact for removal. In this event the find must not come into direct contact with the coatings and must be protected first with acid-free tissue paper or aluminium foil. After the plaster is applied it should be reinforced with securely wound bandages so the block is solid enough to move. This method is more useful for smaller items as the more plaster of Paris is used the heavier the block becomes to move. Lifting should be taken into consideration when plaster of Paris is being used and arrangements for removal put into effect before applying the plaster. Plaster of Paris will generate heat and therefore should not be used on heat-sensitive items. Plaster of Paris may crack if not buffered properly.

An option to reduce the weight when plaster of Paris is used is to dip crepe bandages in the plaster and wrap around the item. Do not use directly on the piece but buffer with aluminium foil or acid-free paper.

If salt encrustations are present on artefacts do not use plaster of Paris as this contains salt (see page 67) which will exacerbate salt damage.

Plaster of Paris can also be used for taking impressions in the soil such as footprints.

MOVING LARGE/HEAVY ITEMS

If using containers to move large or heavy items, prepare them before attempting any removal. Place newspaper in the base to absorb moisture and also to act as a shock absorber, and buffer the sides with newspaper or bubble wrap. Take the container to the object, not vice versa. Identify the weakest points of the item and make sure they will not be in danger when lifting. Protect them with acid-free tissue paper and bubble wrap where necessary. Put a label on the outside of the container and for heavy items add a clear warning as you may not be there when it is lifted again. Always work on the assumption you will not be on site again and leave everything so that someone new does not have to work from scratch.

CONSOLIDATION

Some finds will need to be consolidated, or secured with chemicals before removal. This was done on a site in London when an oyster pit was uncovered which had been lain with rare, early British delph tiles. Removing the tiles caused them to split and crack so they were coated with mesh gauze and a consolidating adhesive. The result was that even though they continued to break apart, all the pieces were left in their exact order to facilitate reconstruction.

It is important that any consolidation chemicals must be water-based in case they need to be removed in the future. If non-soluble chemicals are used there is danger of damage to the item and possible evidence may be lost. This is particularly true if the consolidation is the first application on site. The golden rule when using chemicals or treatment of any kind is keep it to a minimum and never use anything that cannot be reversed. Knowledge and techniques are always increasing and better methods of conservation may be developed, so therefore nothing should be applied to artefacts that will endanger their future.

DEALING WITH FINDS

As finds are being excavated they are usually collected close to the context from which they originated. Most sites provide black plastic garden seed trays for finds to be deposited in as the digger works. These have the advantage of containing the finds, have holes in the base to allow water to drain away and are hard-wearing so can be re-used. It is usually good practice to have several trays near the excavation and finds should be initially sorted into broad categories such as pottery, flint, ceramic building material, metal and bone. This will save time and the finds supervisor will further divide the materials into smaller categories. Heavy items should not be mixed with fragile ones in order to avoid breakages. If no trays are supplied on site then either use a waterproof sheet, a polythene bag or something which will distinguish the pile of finds to prevent people stepping on them.

From the moment finds are added to a tray a context number should be included. Finds from one context should be bagged up before starting a new context and finds from separate contexts should never be mixed. A find that is recorded in situ must have a separate number which tallies with the number given to the find-spot. This number must be included on the context label that accompanies the find. It should also have its position surveyed when recording the context.

Small finds

Complete or fragile items should be taken to the processor immediately if one is on site. Sometimes a find is uncovered that is either fragile, in need of immediate attention or is important and needs to be independently removed. If necessary a photograph will have to be taken in situ, then the exact location recorded, the item bagged separately and a small finds number allocated to it. On some sites where finds are rare all artefacts may be treated as small finds.

4

ON-SITE FINDS RECORDING

As discussed in Chapter One, an artefact is of limited use without its context. Therefore on-site bagging and recording must be clear and concise using materials that have been designed for use in archaeology, with longevity and resistance to decay in mind. Do not use other materials unless absolutely necessary.

WRITING THE LABELS

With each bag of finds a minimum of two context labels should be included. Labels should be made available to the diggers in the finds hut or a convenient place. Make sure the correct Tyvek labels are used; these are made from spun bonded polythene and are tough, waterproof and decay resistant. Avoid writing notes, context details, or information that may be needed later on scraps of paper. Ordinary paper will quickly turn to pulp if allowed to grow damp and unless finds are going to be processed very quickly they could end up in storage for some time. As mentioned in Chapter Two, objects left in the ground for many years achieve a chemical balance with their surrounding matrix. When disturbed this balance is compromised and as a result an artefact could undergo a chemical reaction or simply lose moisture. If finds have to be stored over damp seasons, then any paper inclusions will simply rot. If there is no option but to use paper then place the label in a small bag, staple shut and staple inside the bag of finds so that it does not become damp.

Tyvek was the result of an industrial accident in 1955 but it took a further twelve years to develop and commercialise. It is a construction of random distributed and non-directional fine, white, continuous filaments resulting in a spun-bonded, non-woven, high density polyethylene fabric that is rot-proof, tear resistant, lightweight, strong, waterproof and acid-free. Archaeological units adopted Tyvek due to its longevity and durability, a practice that was then adopted by museums. Elsewhere it is extensively used in envelope manufacture because of its lightness, and in the medical profession due to its ability to resist bacteria.

It shrinks at 118°c and is degraded by turpentine and kerosene.

The recording of information is vital, but what is equally important is that the information survives, so labels must be marked with an ink that will withstand the rigours of excavation and processing. The digger must bear in the mind the future of the label they are writing. As most finds are washed, sometimes with power sprays, the label may get wet and the ink will become saturated.

The correct type of pens should be left in the finds hut by the site supervisors or the finds processor. They should be felt tipped pens which have been researched and tested to ensure their longevity (see page 74). However, sooner or later these will invariably disappear and diggers will resort to using their own. It is vital that diggers using their own pens check that they are definitely waterproof, for example if the ink used produces a pink tinge, stop using the pen immediately as it is not water-proof and the writing will not survive. If a recommended type of pen is not available it is possible to use a ballpoint but again, check the ink is waterproof. Although felt-tipped pens are preferred, one advantage of a ballpoint is that they often need some pressure to write with so that even if the ink does fade the resulting indentation may still be possible to read. Also bear in mind that the ink in most cheap pens is not lightproof and the writing will fade over time.

Do not use a pen with a thick nib as it can be difficult to write legibly on a small label and mis-readings are common, much to the

annoyance of the processor who has then to try and find out which digger was responsible for the label and get it marked up properly. If they
cannot be correctly identified the finds may result in being declared
unstratified and therefore of limited use. If there is difficulty in writing
try and make things as clear as possible, for example use the continental
7 to avoid it becoming confused with the number 1.

Do not use pencil as the writing often becomes illegible over time
and pencil does not photocopy well. Each finds label should include
the initials of the digger. It is a common occurrence through tiredness
or cold to transpose a number or letter. If a mistake does occur it is a
straightforward task to trace the digger to check the information. If not
present the processor has to go through the time-consuming process
of trawling the site records trying to find the information. Often finds
have to be declared unstratified if they cannot be accurately traced to the
correct context. It is therefore worth taking time to ensure that the correct ink is being used because those labels will always be reused by the
processor. If the labels are not suitable they will have to be re-written,
costing time and money.

Site code

This appears on all references to the site and is unique to that site. If a site
code is not included the item can probably never be returned to the relevant collection. The site code will be supplied by the site manager. An
existing code may be used at a later date for the same site even if there
has been a gap in the excavation or if it had previously been used for
the watching brief. This continuity allows records to be stored together.
However, if extensive post-excavation work has been carried out a new
number may be issued to avoid confusion.

Using the label on page 58 as an example:

1) Each label must have the abbreviated site number. In this case
   KEW stands for King Edward building. Where possible the site
   numbers reflect the name of the site such as King Edward, but
   where this is too close to an existing site, a number will be given
   which can bear no relevance to the name of the site. The number
   99 is the year.

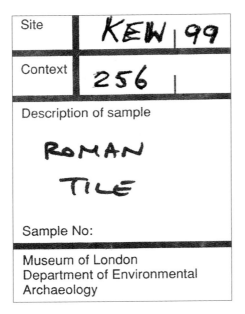

Site	KEW¡99
Context	256 ¡

Description of sample

RoMAN

TILE

Sample No:

Museum of London
Department of Environmental
Archaeology

Finds label

2) The description of the contents. This can be detailed or not, as the digger wishes. Often it can simply say 'pot' or 'Roman pot' or 'Roman Samian pot'.

Always write the type of find on the label so they can be separated quickly. When the finds and bags are muddy it is often impossible to identify the contents without adequate labelling.

This is also the place where warnings should be written such as 'loose glass'. Processors work through bags quickly and if not warned they could easily cut themselves. Always warn when glass or sharp flint, or anything else that can cut the processor is included.

3) Sample No.: shows the number of any samples taken.

4) Some have a small triangle containing a number on them; this is the small finds number relating to the artefact (not present in the illustration). This is the number given to a find recorded in situ (see page 54) such as a grave good.

5) If sieved indicate with the intials BS (bulk sieved) or WS (wet sieved

BAGS

Bags used to hold excavated finds must be durable. Many sites will use zip-lock or self-sealing plastic bags (familiar to many people as freezer bags, see page 37) which are useful as they have white strips to write on and so save context labels. The down-side is that there is a tendency for the zip-lock to part and deposit the contents all over the floor. Such self-sealing bags can only be open a couple of times before losing their watertight ability and, as most bags on site are recycled the more these bags are used the weaker the zip-lock becomes. Some people considerately put a staple at the top to protect against this but this invariably means the bag cannot be re-used. The plastic is so thin it cannot withstand being pulled apart and rips where the staple is removed. The best kind of bags are clear polythene as these are tough, long-lasting and can be repeatedly cleaned out, stapled and recycled. They come in a useful range of sizes, typically 15.25cm x 22.9cm; 20cm x 30.5cm; 30.5cm x 45.7cm; and 45.7cm x 61cm.

BAGGING EXCAVATED FINDS

Bag all finds from one context when that particular context is completely excavated or if it is the end of the day. Do not mix finds in one bag unless absolutely necessary. As it is rarely possible to record finds individually they are collected together and treated as bulk. Pot is always processed first in order to provide spot dates so it needs to be located quickly. Never mix fragile materials with heavier ones. It has been known for glass to be included with building material which, of course, ends up as small fragments. Common sense should prevail.

Bear in mind that many of the bags, once full, may receive quite heavy handed treatment when they are moved around and from the site. Problems can occur when the wrong bags are being used, or the site runs out of certain sizes and diggers have to resort to overstuffing bags. Not only is this a false economy but filling the large sized bags to capacity can contravene health and safety as they may then be too heavy to safely carry. Full bags will also be vulnerable to splitting and jagged items can create holes. Filling the bag so much that only a small strip of plastic can be stapled will, in many cases, result in it bursting open, spilling the contents. When using a recycled bag, shake it to make sure there is nothing in it left behind or that it has no large holes.

If not immediately recovered from a broken bag it is likely most of the finds will be declared unstratified and thrown away thereby negating all the work done to excavate them in the first place and losing the information. It is not an unfamiliar sight to walk into a finds hut and see pieces of pottery lying about the floor, discarded because of poor recovery practices.

Once a sufficient amount of material has been placed in a bag at least two context labels should be filled out (do not write on the polythene bags themselves as few inks are capable of remaining on the polythene surfaces.) Slide the first label down the internal wall of the bag, facing outwards. It is important that the digger place the label so that it can clearly be read without having to open the bag. As a finds supervisor will often be asked to process part or all of a specific context in order to provide spot dating, all finds from this context need to be removed. There is no end of frustration on the part of the processor in having to open numerous bags to turn labels around. If the bag is large and full, add several labels for insurance.

The top of the bag should be rolled over once (at most twice) to the same length of a context label to protect the whole label. The second context label should be included in-between the opening of the bag and facing outwards so it may be easily seen. Do not staple the label to the outside of the bag as it could be torn off whilst bags are being moved around. Secure the label with one staple. It is not advisable to use more than one staple for when the finds processors come to wash the finds they tear the label from the bag in order to re-use it. If it is secured with more than one staple this can cause the label to rip and a new one will have to be provided, wasteful of both time and labels.

Staple the bag so that it is securely closed. Use one staple in the middle for small bags, two for medium ones and three evenly spaced ones for larger bags. Do not staple the whole length of the bag nor roll the top over and over as with wet slippery gloves on it can be almost impossible for processors to open the bags and they will have to waste the bag by cutting it open. Finds can also be stored for long periods of time before being processed and a profusion of rusted staples may discolour the finds inside.

Whole items should be bagged separately and taken to the finds supervisor as soon as possible to avoid any breakages on site.

LABELLING LARGE ITEMS

Where items are too large to be put into a bag, labels can be attached directly to them. Pierce a hole in a Tyvek label and attach with a terylene or polypropylene twine, or plastic garden ties. Try to avoid organic string or rope as these can disintegrate over a period of time, particularly if the item is left outside. It is best, if an item is intended to remain outdoors for an extended period, to place the label inside a small plastic bag and attach the bag to the item. Tie the label loosely around the object using a reef knot. Pull the knot until secure, but do not 'strangle' the piece. If no labels are available write on card or paper and place in a polythene bag made waterproof and secure.

RECORDING EXCAVATED FINDS

Early archaeologists recorded their information in note books; however, this information was often dependent on the individual's interpretations and recording methods. During the 1970s recording was standardised on a pro-forma and the information required was listed in order that nothing would be missed out. This meant the data could be entered on a computer more effectively.

Once finds have been excavated they must be recorded on the dedicated context sheet supplied by the unit. If there are no finds always tick the 'None' box for clarity.

If a find is given a small finds number (see page 58) then it is necessary to include as much information as possible as to its precise location. Often a find will have a particular significance to its context, so it should be plotted on a site plan or photographed in situ. For example at a London site a rare mortaria was found among a blackened layer. From further excavations it could be seen that the vessel must have stood on a shelf which had been burnt along with the rest of the area. The rarity of the mortaria suggests it had been preserved by the occupants and is a good example of a curated object with a date far earlier than the site itself.

PHOTOGRAPHY

Before removing fragile objects it is advisable to photograph them in case they later disintegrate. Not only will this provide a record of what the item looked like but in case of reconstruction it will help the conservator.

If exact measurements are needed a drawing should also be made before lifting. A photograph will not provide exact information such as size and measurements in relation to its surroundings, whereas a drawing will give the exact position recorded on graph paper.

5

FINDS PROCESSING

Finds processors tend to work out their daily schedule according to individual preference but the most logical approach is for them to wash finds in the morning – which means they can keep dry for the rest of the day! The afternoon can then be devoted to recording and/or computing.

Small finds should be examined and cleaned first. Coins and other metal objects should be given priority to avoid any deterioration. If processing on-site, the metal items and coins should be recovered, about an hour before the end of the day, and left out to dry. Try not to leave metal items in bags overnight (in case of condensation), but get them into a dry environment as soon as possible.

A preliminary examination of each item should be made to determine its material, composites and condition, in order to determine a course of action in caring for the piece.

OBSERVING ITEMS

After an item has been excavated if there is any doubt about its stability it is advisable to monitor it, particularly in the days shortly after excavation. All items decay in different ways and at different times according to their own stability and to the environmental effects. If an item begins to change colour or texture after excavation then the corrosion process has been accelerated. This can be seen when copper objects begin to form a light, powdery green coating. When an item is composite, parts may decompose at a different rate to the rest of the piece. Therefore when cleaning a composite item it is important to be aware that some metals may be present only as stains. The rust stains on items such as folding knives may be the only indication of an iron blade. Take care when cleaning and do not scrub too hard on those areas which may contain information regarding missing materials.

PREPARING THE TRAYS

Before washing it is necessary to prepare the trays used to hold finds while they dry. Take a seed tray and line it with clean newspaper, which is highly absorbent and aids the drying process. If there are a number of small finds and drying space and/or trays are in short supply, a way to save on both is to fold the newspaper into a 'concertina' (broadsheets are best for this as they are longer). Fold the paper three or four times so that ridges separate each section. This provides a way to create a physical barrier between finds that prevents both the finds and labels getting mixed up.

PRELIMINARY CLEANING

Prior to washing, scrape off any excess soft mud with a non-metallic implement such as a plastic spoon or wooden coffee stirrer. Plastic or wooden tools reduce the risk of marking the artefact, in fact, the scraper should be of a softer material than that being worked on – this will reduce the risk of marking the artefact. With some soils (such as clay), flicking with the point of a leaf trowel or knife may be more effective, as scraping clay may just smear it around. Another option is to wait until the clay is dry and pick it off with a wooden tool. Preliminary cleaning is particularly useful if finds are being washed in bowls or sinks as it lessens the amount of dirt in the water. Use plastic shopping bags or bin liners to deposit the mud in and then dispose of in a suitable place (anywhere where it won't impede the excavation or water drainage).

Metals should have the surface dirt gently brushed off with a soft brush until the outline is achieved and then a point (such as a dentist point or preferably a wooden plant stick) should be used to pick off some of the encrustation. Before cleaning encrustation it is necessary to bear in mind that the encrustation itself may be important. Often the corrosion can alter the weight, shape and colour of an object and may contain information such as remains of adjacent textiles or, if in the base of a vessel, the remains of the contents. Encrustation may contain information regarding the matrix in which it has laid if it has picked up seeds or pollen. It may also cover any decoration and, by removing the corrosion, the decoration may also be inadvertently removed. Small items that are covered with encrustations may have no core and will therefore be brittle and if subject to rough treatment may fall apart.

When scraping dirt away never use force or pressure as this may place strains on weak areas that are not immediately visible.

Some items should not be cleaned. Where there may be residue in the base of a vessel, such as food remains, this should be left and sieved for environmental evidence. If microware analysis is required on flint, or metal tools, these should not be cleaned.

WATER

Water is present at all times in the atmosphere. It is chemically neutral but rainwater can carry pollutants from industry or domestic use such as coal fires. Domestic water is usually defined as being 'hard' (with many dissolved minerals) or 'soft' (with few dissolved minerals). Hard water has various amounts of calcium sulphate, calcium bicarbonate and magnesium and can usually be easily identified as soap will not lather easily, and 'fur' appears in kettles. It is important therefore not to allow water to gather in pools in parts of the artefact as a residue of minerals can be deposited when the water evaporates. If in any doubt about using domestic water to clean an item either boil it to remove most of the sulphates, use distilled water, or use water that has been treated to exclude all impurities and has a pH of 7.

WASHING

Different artefacts have different washing requirements so refer to the individual materials listed below.

If using a sink take great care about the drainage (see Chapter 2). Do not wash finds under running water as this is not only a great waste of water but it makes the item too wet and fragile, and composite items may be placed under too much strain by the pressure of the water.

If using bowls have two, both of cool or tepid water. Do not use hot water as the heat may damage the artefact. One bowl is used for washing and one for rinsing, but keep all artefacts out of the water as much as possible; the more sodden a piece, the longer it will take to dry. The water in the first bowl should be changed as often as possible as washing in dirty water may leave smear marks. Changing the water regularly on certain sites may be difficult if the water supply is limited – in these circumstances keep a separate bowl of water with a clean cloth which can be used to wash away any smears or marks.

Most finds can be washed with a soft toothbrush or nailbrush. However, the brush technique used should be adapted according to the item being washed. Keep a watchful eye on the item being cleaned and adapt the pressure and method according to the results on the artefact. Pottery in particular often suffers from overzealous washing and too rigorous a clean will not only result in 'having the life scrubbed out of it' (a common criticism by pottery specialists of inexperienced washing) but also in the removal of any decoration or details that may be present. Wood and leather should never be washed with a brush of any kind as this will leave striations on them. They should be washed with a sponge or gently with the fingers. It may be useful to break up the sponge into smaller pieces for easier use. Do not use any soaps as the chemical content will, generally be unknown and may cause damage to the finds. Soaps produce bubbles and these can sometimes obscure details on the items which may need careful treatment.

If the piece is fragile or composite it may be washed with a sponge. The advantage of a sponge is that it is soft enough not to damage most artefacts. If an object is too friable and it is breaking up, it may be better to place it in a bag, punch some holes to keep it ventilated and leave it for conservation. This will avoid any accidental loss of small parts.

If an item is composite or fragile, clean it over a screen of mesh or plastic so that if any pieces are dislodged they will not be lost. Also, adhesives used in the past have been made to many different recipes and may no longer be stable – so as the adhesive dissolves the piece will fall apart. This is more likely to happen if the water is too hot.

If paint work can be seen on any artefacts do not wash them. In a small test area brush the dirt away very gently or use a blow brush to blow off the excess dirt. If the paint becomes detached stop at once and send to a conservation lab.

Never pick up complete items by handles, points or other protuber-ances but lift, with two hands if necessary, below the centre of gravity (usually at its thickest and therefore strongest part). It is almost impos-sible to know if an object has suffered internal damage and has cracks or strains which are not noticeable to the naked eye. By picking up items by handles or points these strains may give way. Take care when lifting items whilst wearing damp or wet gloves as these can be very slippery.

Once the piece has been cleaned lay it to dry on sheets of newspaper.

Once a context has been processed the bags containing the excavated finds should be washed out and sent back to the finds hut for re-use by the diggers.

SALT ENCRUSTATION

Those items recovered from a salt enriched ground may develop a layer of salt crystals as the piece begins to dry. This salt encrustation may cause surface flaking and, in severe cases, can destroy the piece. Salt-covered small finds should be removed to the processing area as soon as possible to be cleaned.

Salt can crystallise when it is removed from its matrix and this may take place so quickly that the piece may break apart, particularly if exposed to the sun. Artefacts that do have salt encrustation should be kept out of the sun and allowed to dry slowly and the salt gently brushed off in order to make the object stable. If the piece is relatively stable it should be washed clean of the salt with distilled water (as most local waters will contain salt themselves). Immerse the piece in a clean plastic container of distilled water for a day or longer depending on the encrustation. Then remove it, allow the piece to dry slowly, brush off the salt and, if the salt has not been removed, immerse the piece again. Keep doing this until there are no more salt crystals. If not all of the salt has been removed a note needs to accompany the piece stating this, so that the conservators can continue the treatment.

CLEANING DRY FINDS

If there is only a covering of light dust a hand-held vacuum cleaner can be used. These are available from many commercial outlets and generally come with a range of brush sizes and nozzles. When using the nozzles a covering of muslin or similar material must be used to prevent any loose items being sucked in.

For gentle brushing always use high-quality brushes as cheap ones will shed bristles which could cause damage when retrieving them from inside an artefact. Never exert pressure on the item lest it be marked – the brush should flick the dirt away, not actually brush it. Once a brush becomes wet, dirt will cling to it rendering it useless, as it can end up depositing more dirt than it removes. Wash brushes regularly and use brushes with white bristles to see when dirty or if anything has been caught in the bristles.

Another useful brush is the photographer's puffer brush. Not only does it have soft bristles but the occasional squirt of air will remove additional dust.

DRYING

Different artefacts will have different drying times, even if they are recovered from the same context. This may be due to a number of reasons: they may have been constructed differently; adhesives used may be of a different composition; one object may have been generally treated differently from the other; or it may have been subject to different environmental influences when buried. Therefore do not assume that all objects recovered together will dry at the same rate.

Items which naturally contain moisture will be those most affected by over-drying. Wood and ivory will warp and split and veneers or inlays may lift. Other materials such as stone or pottery may begin to crumble. Do not leave the object in direct sunlight as strong light will heat the object above the temperature of the room and can cause damage or condensation.

Bulk finds

When drying bulks finds place them in suitable containers. For large amounts of bulk ceramic finds bread crates are recommended as they can hold large volumes, are strong and have carrying handles on each side. They can also be stacked.

For smaller bulk finds the 'mushroom' crates used by fruit and vegetable sellers are ideal. These are plastic, usually blue, lattice styled containers. Most fruit and veg sellers throw them away at the end of the day so they can often be scrounged for free. The lattice work provides a good air flow, they are very light and are designed to stack one on top the other. These have often proved invaluable because they can be stacked quite high and quite safely (unless of course building materials are stacked in them in which case they have been known to buckle!). They should be lined in the bottom with clean newspaper to absorb as much of the water as possible.

Small finds

Small finds are placed in seed trays. Propping stable items alongside the tray edges will allow a greater circulation of air and they will dry quicker than if they were laid flat. Include two context labels. Ideally these should be the ones already made out by the diggers on site, but if they are not suitable (for example because they are illegible or have been filled out with non-waterproof pen), new ones will have to be made out. One label should be placed in the tray amongst the finds, with the other propped up alongside the narrower tray edge. This way, when the tray is placed on a ledge the context number or finds description can be quickly seen without having to recover labels from each tray.

Include a small scrap of paper with the finds displaying the washing date – this will serve as a monitor of drying times and allow the processor to be able to predict when items may be ready.

All trays should then be placed in an area where they will not be disturbed, and where there will be a consistent heat source, for at least 24 hours.

BAGGING

Check finds are complete dry before bagging. If they are not mould can develop and the washing process will have to be repeated. If large numbers of sherds are placed in one bag it may be useful to perforate the bag to avoid the build-up of condensation. Some bags do come ready perforated but if not it is an easy job to punch holes in the bags, either with a penknife or using a stationery hole punch.

Bagging up should be done according to the guidelines regarding bagging on site, already discussed (see page 59). One context label should be included in the body of the bag – slide it down the wall of the bag, facing outwards. Fold the top of the bag over once, at most twice, and include a second label under the outer fold, facing outwards so it can be seen. Staple the label once, and then staple the fold so that the bag is securely closed. Do not add too many staples as this will make the bags difficult to open – and, as the bags will also be opened several times, over-stapling will quickly ruin them.

Whole items should be bagged separately. If items have protrusions which need protecting, wrap with acid-free tissue paper and then cover will bubble wrap. Do not write on the bags themselves as few inks can remain intact on polythene.

With bulk items it may be useful to throw in a few more labels so that even if they move around inside the bag it is not too difficult to find at least one of them. Never leave bagged items in sunlight as this will cause condensation.

Accessioned finds

Accessioned finds (finds which are considered worthy of further study, are given individual numbers and are packed individually) must be bagged separately. All accessioned finds should be placed in a bag with a backing of acid-free polyethylene foam cut to the internal size of the bag. The find should then be placed securely in the bag facing outwards so it can be clearly seen to avoid having to open the bag. If the artefact is fragile and could move around too much in the bag then acid-free tissue paper should be added to keep it immobile and avoid possible damage. Once the find is secure bend the bag backwards so that the top reaches the bottom (or as close as possible without straining the bag or the find). Place a context label inside the two flaps and staple as before. The bags will then be placed in storage boxes and need to be of a uniform size and shape in order for quick reference.

Acid-free (also referred to as inert or lignin free)

Always use approved archival materials on or close to objects. These can be purchased from conservation suppliers. Normal everyday stationery such as paper, card and tissue is usually made from either wood or cotton and therefore has a base of cellulose fibre pulp which is naturally acidic. Unless this acid is neutralised it will eventually degrade the paper, turning it yellow and making it brittle and weak. Most people will be familiar with the brown, brittle appearance of old newspapers. Papers which have a pH of 5 and below are considered highly acidic so to combat this, manufacturers neutralise the acids with chemicals such as calcium carbonate. Even this however is a temporary solution, as within 5-10 years the natural acids will re-emerge and the paper reverts back to its acidic state. (Museums often change their packaging every 5-10 years.) To get around this some manufacturers overbuff the treatment and raise it to a high alkaline level of around 8.5pH (for more on pH see page 15). Whilst this alkalinity is suitable for most objects it may be harmful to others so it is advisable to check with the manufacturers as to the pH content of the 'acid-free' materials being used. For safety it is advisable to acquire materials as close to a pH of 7 (or neutral) as possible as these will remain inert for longer. The best materials are those made from Manila hemp and, whilst expensive, this is recommended for very sensitive artefacts such as fabrics and photographs.

Bagging artefacts in water

When bagging with water place the item in a bag larger than the item to be included, and then cover with cool, clean water. Do not 'drown' the item but cover sufficiently with water. Too much water will make handling the bag difficult and increases the risk of ruptures. Include a context label making absolutely sure that the label has been written with a waterproof pen and that it faces outwards (as it is annoying to be forced to open the bag if it is being heat sealed).

Fold the bag over and expel as much of the air as possible. If a heat sealer is available, use it to seal the bag. Place the sealer clear of the water and make sure the whole line is tightly shut otherwise the water will leak. Place a second label above the sealed line and inside the top part of the bag, then heat seal a second line above the label. Heat sealing two lines provides a double security in case the first seal leaks. Once the bag is sealed place it inside a second larger dry bag and staple shut as before. If no heat sealer is available plastic, food containers can be used, or as a last resort, staples the bag.

Bags of wet finds should be stored in a damp box, stout crates, large plastic rubbish bins or plastic washing-up bowls to keep the bags secure. Cover whenever possible with a lid or if no lid is available then use black bin liners to keep out the light and prevent the growth of mould. Check the bags regularly to monitor any mould growth and, if necessary, change the water.

Do not use fungicides as these are merely palliative and it is not recommended by conservators (despite the advice given in a number of archaeological excavation books). The amounts needed vary greatly according to the weight per volume of organic materials to water, and the calculations needed are complex. In addition, the addition of fungicide, which often goes un-recorded, can be a danger to those working on the pieces in the future.

BOXING

Crystal boxes
If placing a find in a plastic box use acid-free tissue paper to support it. Crumple the paper and make a 'nest' in the centre of the box surrounded by packing material so that the item cannot move. The paper has to be arranged so that the object can be seen (to avoid constantly opening the box), but also held securely in place. Place a layer of acid-free tissue paper on top so that if the box is accidentally inverted the item should be so secure that it will not bang against the lid and become damaged. The box should then be placed in a bag and labelled accordingly. Make sure there is a label within the box in case it becomes separated from its bag. Do not place the label at the bottom of the box making it necessary to turn the box upside down to view it, but if possible fold and place down the side.

Boxing/bagging metals
Once thoroughly dried metal items should be bagged as above and placed in a sturdy plastic Tupperware, or Stewart box. If necessary the

Flint core packed in acid-free
tissue paper, in a plastic food
container

inside of the box should be layered with acid-free polyethylene foam
and/or acid-free tissue paper, packed to prevent the item from moving.

A sachet of silica gel will need to be added. Silica gel acts as a desiccant
by absorbing moisture in humid conditions and releasing moisture in
dry conditions without ever becoming moist itself, but it is only effective in a sealed environment. It is used to control humidity levels in
storage containers and display cases and these days is often found in the
packaging of commercial electronic and photographic equipment. Silica
gel can be bought loose, as sachets of white granules, or as blue granules
which turn to pink when complete absorption has taken place. The gel
can usually be regenerated in a standard oven at 100-200°C. An alternative to silica gel is 'Art-Sorb' which comes as beads or sheets or in two
sizes of sealed cassettes.

The gel needs to be monitored regularly and changed if necessary.
The wetter the piece the more often the gel will need to be changed.
If coloured gel is not available, include a humidity indicator strip along
the inside wall of the box so that it is visible from the outside. A humidity strip is a piece of blotting paper impregnated with cobalt chloride
and divided into nine coloured sections (from blue through lavender to
pink) that will indicate the relative humidity (RH) of the surrounding
air. When the top section turns to pink the silica gel needs replacing. The
range of accuracy is 10-80 per cent (+/-5 per cent). Never allow silica

gel to come into direct contact with an artefact as this means the moisture will be touching the item instead of being kept away.

Take care when stacking the boxes. If too much pressure is placed on
them the lids will buckle, allowing air in and making the silica gel useless. To ensure the box is as air tight as possible once it has been packed,
tape down the lid with masking tape.

If boxes are not available use polyethylene bags – place the item in
one bag with a smaller, perforated bag to hold the silica gel. The gel must
not in any way touch the item. Never put metal items in bags without
silica gel because of the risk of condensation.

Acid-free boxes
Boxes containing bagged artefacts should be acid-free. When packing
the lids should fit securely on top and there should be no protrusions
that will cause the box to buckle or the item to be damaged. Do not
place too many boxes on top of each other as the weight will buckle the
lowest one. If there are a number of pieces which belong to one item or
one collection mark the boxes to indicate this, such as 1 of 3, 2 of 3, 3 of
3 so that it is clear how many boxes there are.

LABELLING LARGE OBJECTS

When an object is too large to either bag or box a label needs to be tied
firmly to it, according to notes on page 70.

WRITING THE LABELS

A staff member at MoLSS (Museum of London Specialist Services) has
conducted extensive research into pen use on labels. She chose a number
of brands and used them to write the labels which were then placed in
water and checked regularly over a year. Only the writing from one pen,
the Berol, was still legible a year later. The processing of finds a year later
is not an unusual event. Often a site can run out of funds and so processing is fitted in when and if it can be done. Therefore as a rule of thumb
stick to pens that are known to work such as the Berol, Autoseal Ink,
Staedtler or Artline.

CROSSMENDING POTTERY

For a number of reasons, such as archaeological open days, it may be necessary to reconstruct a whole pot from its sherds. Reconstructing a pot, or cross mending, is the piecing together of a single vessel from the sherds regardless of where the sherds were found. Reconstructing a vessel is only done when absolutely necessary and usually only for temporary means as whole pots take up too much storage and are weaker and therefore more likely to break. To hold the vessel together for a short period of time, such as the taking of photographs, then masking tape may be used. Glue should only be used if vessels are to be exhibited. If a piece is reconstructed it is useful to number the pieces in case it needs to be redone.

When reconstructing pottery it is advisable to do so over a sand/soil tray so that the sand/soil can be moulded into shapes that will stabilise the pot as it is being constructed. As most sites will be unable to use sand trays or firm enough clean soil then using acid-free tissue paper may be better. To give added strength plasticine could be applied to the interior to give it strength but do not press hard against the walls of the vessel in case they break.

END OF THE DAY

All finds must be removed on the same day as recovery if possible. If left exposed overnight or on weekends the finds may became damaged by weather conditions or be disturbed by animals or people. Finds should be placed in the finds hut if one is present, or in a secure place. All finds should be bagged and labelled (see Chapter 3) then placed in separate piles, i.e. place all pottery bags together, all building material together, etc.

6

MATERIALS

GENERAL PRINCIPLES

The materials described below often require individual types of care. However, there are two guidelines applicable to them all:

If an object is found broken, bent or distorted do not try to restore it, as more damage may be caused by attempting to manipulate it back into what is assumed to be the original shape. Objects have more value in their recovered state as evidence of their history and the damage has a story to tell.

Composites – treat the whole item according to its most fragile part. Look out for rivets and avoid getting them wet as corrosion can increase their size and force breaks into the surrounding materials.

The treatments listed below are basic and, if there is any doubt, a conservator should be contacted.

ALABASTER

Alabaster is a form of gypsum (hydrated calcium sulphate) similar in appearance to marble with colours that range from a creamy white (very rare) through pink, red and green to a dark honey brown. It has a sugary, friable surface, is soft enough to be cut with a penknife, and slightly soluble in water which makes it unsuitable for external use. It is also a weak stone and therefore does not have the strength to be used as building material. However, the ease with which it can be carved made it ideal for detailed decorative work such as tomb sculptures and panels and its unique translucent quality makes it valuable for decorative work such as vases. During the late fourteenth century deposits were found in Nottingham and this became an area of high production, with wares being exported from Iceland to Spain. However, due to the high demand the product was often poor. There was a great revival of alabaster carving during the Victorian era and a 'streaky bacon' look alabaster was very popular. Most statuary alabaster is found in churches as funerary monuments and funerary accessories but numerous small objects, such as household ornaments were also made from alabaster.

Survival
Alabaster will survive in alkaline soils, but as with other sulphates and carbonates it reacts with acids so will not readily survive in acid soils.

Care
Soft stones such as alabaster, marble and limestone easily absorb dirt but even very dirty alabaster will usually clean up well and, unlike marble, it rarely stains. Do not use any kind of chemicals as alabaster can be attacked by acids and will effervesce. Do not soak or wash in running water as, being a soft stone, it may disintegrate.

Up until the beginning of the seventeenth century alabaster monuments were often painted so they should be carefully examined before washing to avoid losing any paint layers. If paint is flaking it should be possible to consolidate it with Paraloid but check with a conservator before applying.

If gloves are not available wash hands before handling soft stones like marble or alabaster to avoid grease transferring onto the stone.

Heat from sunlight can damage large-grained alabaster so do not leave out to dry in sunlit areas.

AMBER

Amber (also called succinite) is a fossilised form of tree resin originally exuded to protect the tree against disease, insects and wounds. There are only about 20 places in the world where quality amber can be found, the most important deposits being from the Baltic which are commonly between 25 and 50 million years old.

Carved amber exists from the prehistoric period and one of the oldest known examples is from Cheddar caves in Somerset, England, where beads have been dated to the Lower Palaeolithic (11000-9000 BC). However, it was from the Neolithic (4000-1900 BC) that trade in amber began to become widespread so that by the Bronze Age there were established 'amber routes' which covered Europe and extended into the Far East.

Amber is commercially used as a gemstone (although, along with pearl, coral and jet it is not of a mineral origin) and is the lightest substance used for jewellery. It is often found in necklaces or in rings although it has been used for other works of art, perhaps the most famous being the Amber Room of Russia which was lost to fire in the Second World War.

Identification

Amber is a translucent material with a glossy shine and over 250 clas-sifications of colours ranging from black to white, with some rare blues and greens. Some pieces are cloudy due to the inclusion of microscopic droplets of water. The most common colour is a light to dark yellow that darkens to a red-brown with age. Under a ultra-violet lamp it will fluoresce green. Pieces can be full of small cracks, blemishes or inclusions such as insects, although the latter are rare. It is relatively soft material, 2-2.5 on the Mohs scale and can be scratched with a finger nail. It is brittle and the surface chips not peels. It feels warm to the touch and is combustible, being easily ignited with just a cigarette lighter – when burnt gives off a pleasant aromatic scent. Similarly when carved it gives off a pleasant odour and forms a white powder.

When rubbed vigorously amber becomes electrically charged, and will attract small light items such as lint. Consequently the Greek word for amber is *electron* – the origin of the word electricity. It is very light in weight and will float in salty water but sink in fresh water. This is an important factor in its distribution as it has floated to other locations including Britain. Plastic amber beads are harder than the real thing and do not have the ability to be electrically charged.

When badly deteriorated amber can be hard to distinguish from soil and in this state can easily crumble on removal.

Survival

Amber is a relatively unstable material as it oxidises on exposure to air and is sensitive to light – it decays slowly but constantly. Due to this instability it is preserved only in certain circumstances, such as in dense wet sediments like peat. As it decays the surface darkens, and cracks will appear which will continue to widen. The surface will then appear rough and crumbly and begin to fall apart unless it is conserved. The conservation of amber has proved difficult for most museums.

Care

Keep as found so if recovered wet, keep wet as drying may cause the piece to craze and become opaque. If wet and fragile lift with its surrounding matrix and keep slightly damp and in a bag – store in a cool dark place until removal for conservation. If amber is dry do not wet but softly brush (if the piece is stable). If the piece has many fine cracks do not clean.

The origin of a piece of amber can be sourced using infra-red chromatography (however this is expensive). It is essential that no chemicals such as those found in cleaning products are used prior to sourcing as this will interfere with the process and invalidate the results.

Do not pack or store amber with any other items, even other amber pieces as, being a soft material, it is prone to chipping. This is the reason amber beads are always threaded with a knot between each bead. Heat, such as hot water, may shatter the item, as will very cold water. Chemicals such as washing liquids will interact with amber and may form a permanent dull, or whitening of the surface. Do not place near a heat source, or direct light, to dry out as this may cause cracks. Amber dissolves in many common solvents, so those who handle or wear amber jewellery should always put it on after using chemicals such as hairspray or perfume as these will create a white coating over the amber which cannot be removed.

ANTLER

Together with ordinary bone, antler was one of the 'plastics' of early eras because of its strength and flexibility. It is stronger and more versatile than bone, especially when carving – antler can be carved in many directions whereas bone usually has to be carved with the grain in order to give it strength. It is for this reason that most combs are made from antler and not bone (as is popularly believed).

Antler is a form of bone which grows on the head of a variety of deer. The core of an antler is a spongy tissue which rarely survives as it is fragile when exposed. This spongy core was used as the basis of early soap. The thickness of the antler varies between species.

Antler was used from the earliest of times – it would have been taken from animals killed for food, but would also have been collected after the deer had shed the antler (usually in January and February). Antler was used for a variety of purposes including harpoons, but was particularly popular as handles for knives and other utensils as the grooved surface provided a good grip. Antler may have been left in its natural white state, or was coloured or stained with dyes. The golden age of antler and bone carving was during the ninth to twelfth centuries.

Red deer are the most common deer in the world and so their antlers are the most commonly used. Characteristic are the rough surface grooves which are the channels along which blood vessels ran to feed the outer skin, or velvet. British red deer often have up to 12-14 tines – small protuberances which could be cut up to make toggles. Unlike the fallow, reindeer and elk there is no palmatation, or broad spreads.

Fallow deer were introduced into Britain in the eleventh century, probably by the Normans. The antler surface is smooth and has no grooves like those on the red deer antler. They have areas of smooth, flattened surfaces known as palmate.

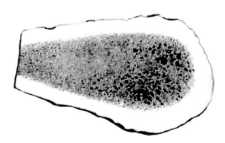

Interior core of antler

Roe deer were in Britain from prehistoric times but declined during the medieval period. It is a small animal, about the size of a large goat, and only the males have antlers, which rise in an almost straight line from the head with a couple of tines on the top. The antler surface is covered with tiny bony nodules.

Reindeer antler was used extensively in the prehistoric times but disappears in Britain around the Mesolithic. The antlers occur on both sexes and consist of a stem which sweeps backwards and upwards and terminates on the upper points as palmates. There are usually two sets, one in the front and one at the back. The surface is smooth with shallow grooves.

Elk disappeared from Britain during the Mesolithic. The antlers have enormous palmates at right angles to the animal's face and the points that surround the palmate point upwards. These broad palmates were ideal for use as shovels.

Decay of antler
Antler survives well in the ground with the exception of acidic soils.

Processing of antler
Keep as found so if recovered wet, keep wet for, if allowed to dry out it may shrink and distort. If dry and stable, it can be lightly washed (do not immerse) and air-dried. Take care when processing composite items as association with materials such as metals can stain antler.

BONE

Bone was used from the earliest times to the late twentieth century when its use was largely replaced by plastics. Bone is often a dense material that can be worked in various ways, the simplest being to whittle with a knife. It cannot be moulded or bent (like horn) and it cannot be worked across the grain as it loses it strength. Bone was easily available although many of the choicest were not available, having been broken up for their valuable marrow used extensively in cooking. The list of different items made from bone is long and varied, and bone was also used for decorative mounts and inlays for boxes and furniture, etc. Wider expanses of bone such as shoulder blades were used to punch out buttons or beads.

Practice decoration on a femur

Most of the bone used was from domesticates such as horses, pigs and sheep although the most commonly used bone was the cattle femur (thigh bones), as these were freely available and had enough bone to be used for making most objects. The head of the femur could be used for spindle weights.

Ribs were often used by potters to burnish pot surfaces and other bone objects were used for culinary purposes as it did not taint the taste of the food. Spoons for boiled eggs and mustard were traditionally made from bone. Due to its accessibility, most families would have bone to make utilitarian objects with. As such, pins and needles, gaming pieces such as counters and dice – which led to the phrase 'rolling the bones' were made from bone.

Bird bones were used for decorating pottery in the prehistoric periods and making musical pipes and whistles. Whale bone could be scavenged from beaches and used for larger items. Even human skull was used to make flat objects.

Bones – animal

Although (strictly speaking) animal bones should come under environmental processing, it is usually the finds processor who deals with them. Faunal analysis, the study of animal bones, is an important area of study covering diet, the socio-economic status of the inhabitants, butchering practices, economy and development of animals. When processing bones be alert for cut marks which may indicate butchery practice.

Some bones may appear to be natural but may have been used by humans, for example potters would often use ribs to smooth the surface of pots.

Articulated animals bones should be recorded and photographed in situ before removing. Finer bones such as fish bones are most often recovered during sieving.

Bones – cremations

For most of history bones were burnt in cremations long enough to make them sufficiently brittle to be broken up and put into a container. This low heat rarely destroyed all of the bone and, although the shape often remains, it is white and very fragile. Bone burnt at a high temperature is also white and fragile, but becomes twisted.

Identification

The colour is naturally a creamy white but it can be dyed other colours. If burnt bone becomes mottled from white to grey or black. In the ground it can take on different shades of brown or black and may show discolouration if in association with metals such as copper or iron. A characteristic feature of many bones is the spongy tissue that appears on the concave surfaces.

Survival

Bone survives reasonably well in many archaeological deposits although it disintegrates quickly in acidic soils. In waterlogged sites bone can be reduced to a sponge-like material. In arid conditions they can become dry, brittle and fragmented.

Care

Wash bone in tepid water with a soft brush and air dry. If thin or fragile pieces are wet when they are recovered, do not allow them to dry out as they will shrink and distort. Take care with composite items and be alert for staining, which will indicate the presence of other materials such as metals.

Do not:
- leave in the sun to dry as it may cause bleaching.
- use metal tools as these can scratch the bone.

- wash vigorously as this may leave marks and may obliterate marks such as butchery cuts.
- wrap in materials such materials, such as cotton wool that can snag on jagged edges - use materials such as bubble wrap or acid-free tissue paper.
- wrap acid-free tissue paper or any other wrapping too tightly as it may cause damage.

Bone is easily warped by heat and will decompose if left too long in water. If bone does swell it will do so across the grain rather than along it.

BRICK

Bricks are made of mud or clay, mixed with a variety of other materials including flint, stones, shells and straw to provide temper and colour.

Identification
Both the brick itself (in terms of composition, colour and shape) and the way bricks are laid together – the bond – can be used for identification. However, in finds processing it is usually single or part bricks that are being processed.

Old bricks can be difficult to date, especially handmade examples as these are subject to many variations. However, the following provides some general guidelines to periods.

Roman brickwork
Roman bricks are smaller than later examples, looking more like thick tiles. Many were re-used in later ages.

Medieval brickwork
During the medieval period many bricks were imported from Flanders, as ballast in wool ships. English bricks were larger, about 280-330mm x 125-150mm x 45-70mm and the earliest known examples are at Abbey at Coggeshall near Colchester, Essex (1220). Bricks were made in many villages and towns, and even large houses had their own clay pits.

In the thirteenth century Flemish brick makers settled on the east coast and brought their production methods – the earliest of these bricks can be found at Little Wenham Hall, near Ipswich, Suffolk (1275). They made small bricks in moulds of a size that easily fit a man's hand to speed laying. They used sand in the mould, so the underside of bricks can have a rough finish. The brick makers did not always fill the moulds properly, so the bricks were not always consistent; consequently, in 1571 regulations were introduced that standardised the size to 22.9cm 11.4cm x 6.35cm (becoming known as 'statute bricks').

Georgian brickwork 1714-1830

The manufacture of brick was greatly improved in the late seventeenth and early eighteenth centuries. Blended clay was used, along with better moulding techniques and more even firing. These allowed bricks of a more consistent shape and size – initially 209mm x 101mm x 63mm, rising to 234mm x 114mm x 114mm in 1784, although in 1803 it was changed again to 228mm x 114mm x76mm.

The colours of bricks were subject to fashion – bright colours such as red and purple as well as grey, were replaced in the 1730s with more subdued browns and pinks. Grey returned as the colour of choice in the mid-eighteenth century, but by 1800 the yellow marl or malm 'London Brick' became widespread as the colour mimicked natural stone and was considered more suitable for the popular classical facades.

Victorian Bricks 1830-1914

In the Victorian period brick manufacturing processes improved still further and bricks became both cheap and highly standardised. Bricks were used to build the huge infrastructure of bridges, canals, factories and cheap housing. More bricks were laid during this period than during all previous periods.

Bricks were now produced using machine presses that ensured consistency in size and shape – the join between bricks could now be much narrower, down to 8mm. Better firing practice allowed the manufacture of very strong, dense bricks suitable for heavy load-bearing projects such as bridges and tunnels. The range of colours available was increased, and the new machines allowed bricks to have a wide variety of profiles at a reasonable cost – so 'weather-struck' and 'cut' style of joins became popular. The transport network that bricks helped to build allowed bricks to be carried over wide areas, and brick making began to be concentrated into a few major manufacturing areas; local variations in brick began to disappear.

One of the most important sources of information in this field is the British Geological Survey (BGS) as it maintains a comprehensive archive of the geology of Britain's building stones.

Survival
Brick is generally a robust material and survives well, although it can be chipped or broken. Rust from any metal associated with the bricks, such as wall ties, can damage brick, and older bricks may have poor protection against water penetration.

Care
Early handmade brick can disintegrate in water so it is important to take care when washing. Record any markings on bricks which may indicate manufacturer or provide other information.

CHARCOAL

When organic material is not completely burnt to ash it remains as a charcoal. It is useless to most life forms (except humans) and is usually left intact, unless destroyed by elements in the soil. Collection does not usually take place unless instructed to do so. If the piece is large enough it may still have enough of the grain to able to provide evidence of the species. Charcoal can be used for radio carbon dating but if selected for this it cannot be handled – surgical gloves must be used. It also must not be touched with metal tools, so use plastic or wooden ones. Store in polythene bags and do not bring it into contact with paper as acid from the paper can damage the piece.

Identification
Charcoal is a black to grey material similar to its original form of wood and found in any place where burning has taken place.

Survival
Charcoal survives in most places but it can be very fragile and upon collection may easily break up.

Care
Keep dry and never introduce it to water.

COPPER

Identification

Pure copper is a shiny reddish metal, but unless cleaned regularly it quickly oxidises and a green patina forms. Copper is usually identified by this patina, which can range from a smooth coating to a thicker encrustation of oxidised metal. The patina is usually stable, but where the metal has a high lead content pitting may occur where the lead has been leached out by the rain.

The common copper alloys are bronze (copper and tin) and brass (copper and zinc). Bronze was the main metal in use until the fifth century BC when iron was introduced. Iron was then used for utilitarian purposes whereas copper alloys were still employed for those items which could be more decorative. Copper items were often gilded or plated with tin, silver or gold which may be not immediately apparent on recovery, as they can appear to be pure silver or gold artefacts. Brass has been found from the Iron Age however it was not until zinc was imported from the sixteenth century that brass become mass-produced.

Where items are particularly corroded there may be a second purple layer of cuprous oxide and cuprous-chloride just below the surface of the original metal. This layer needs to be removed by conservators in a controlled manner to prevent it falling apart.

Survival

Copper alloys will survive well in alkaline and neutral soils but not in acidic ones. The most common colour of copper alloys when recovered is a dark green. If particularly corroded there also may be a thick green encrustation which may obscure the original shape or details.
Other patinas can be found:

- A whitish-grey patina usually indicates a high lead or tin alloy.
- Black and shiny or bright shiny gold-coloured patinas (with possibly some pitting) are usual when recovering from waterlogged conditions.
- Light green patina, powdery with dark spots and flaky indicates corrosion is advancing.

Severe corrosion will include hard warts and blisters with pitting. If the powder is under the surface and in the pits this is known as 'bronze disease' which needs to be arrested as soon as possible. Handle as carefully as possible as items with bronze disease can be extremely fragile.

Care

Do not wash items but if recovered damp or wet then leave to air-dry. Dry earth can be lightly brushed away with a camera lens or makeup brush or with a wooden tool. Pack in polythene bags with a backing of polyethylene foam and then place in a plastic storage box with silica gel and a humidifier strip.

Copper and copper alloys should be stored at an RH of below 35 per cent. If the corrosion is stable leave it alone as removal could do more damage to the artefact and can result in a pitted surface.

CORAL

Coral is the skeletal remains of polyp colonies of the warmer seas, such as the Mediterranean, and consist mainly of calcium carbonate. It is often used for ornament and can be cut and polished into intricate shapes. Coral was well known in the Iron Age for prestige goods and a sword of the La Tene type I (fourth to fifth century BC) has discs of coral embedded in the handle. During the medieval periods Crucifixion crosses were often made from pieces of branched coral – coral 'trees'. In the fourteenth century a necklace of coral was thought to assist in childbirth. It was kept as a charm against thunder and lightning, imprisonment and defeat in battle. In Italy during the seventeenth and eighteenth centuries whole villages were dedicated to producing coral beads, each village making a particular bead. The Victorians would use a sprig of coral as a ring stand – this was later copied in ceramics.

Coral is 4 on the Mohs scale so is soft and easily worked and can be carved with the side of a coin.

Identification

The deep red coral is rarer than the pink, which was very popular with the Victorians.

Survival

Coral does not survive well in waterlogged sites or acid soils.

Care
Due to its softness coral should not be cleaned with metal tools or stored with other items which may damage it. Do not wet or allow it to come into contact with any chemicals as they will cause damage.

ENAMEL

Enamel is a hard form of glass fused onto the surface of objects and can be either opaque or translucent. Enamel is usually divided into three types: champlevé, cloisonné and painted.

Identification
Champlevé is from the French *champs* meaning field and *levé* meaning lifted or raised and consists of cells cut into metal and then filled with enamel paste which, when heated, rise to the surface of the metal. This method was well established by the Celts who used a predominance of red coloured enamel. Romano-British usage included blue, white, green and red enamels. Champlevé fell out of favour until the twelfth century when it was influenced by Byzantine tastes. Limoges in France became the most important centre and most museums contain items from Limoges.

Cloisonné is the oldest form of enamelling and consists of cells made from applying soldering wire onto the surface and filling them with enamel paste. Cloisonné use began about 4,000 years ago and was used extensively in China from the sixteenth century. In the West it regained popularity from the nineteenth century.

Painted – the design painted in colours on an enamel background.

Survival
Enamel will generally survive in the same manner as other glass (see page 92).

Care
Enamels can be washed with warm water and a soft brush, but as most are attached to metals the metals should not be made wet. When cleaning, take care in case pieces of the enamel are loose. Therefore wash or clean over a gauze or cloth so that if any pieces do become detached they will not become lost.

Lithics

FLINTS

Lithics (flint tools and debitage) are the most commonly recovered flints. Also found are gun flints – from the seventeenth to the nineteenth century these were made in their thousands in Britain and exported all over the world.

Identification
Flint is a hard stone which appears most often in a deep shiny black colour, although other colours exist such as red, brown and yellow. Some pieces may have an outer covering (cortex) still adhering to the side. Burnt flint is white or grey and appears with crazed lines.

Survival
Flint survives well in most conditions although burnt flint can be fragile, particularly if recovered from waterlogged conditions.

Care
Most flints can be washed with toothbrushes and clean water. Flint can chip easily so do not store flint tools together but accession separately. Do not store in proximity to metals or other hard objects which may damage the flint.

If any flints have been collected for microwear analysis (to find traces of animal tissues or plant starches which will indicate the use of the tool) do not wash and do not touch the edges.

If burnt flint is stable it can be washed with a soft brush. If it is not stable do not wash as if left in water it can disintegrate.

GEMSTONE JEWELLERY

Gems come in numerous colours and varieties and are too varied to go into detail here. Below are a few general guidelines for gems and the jewellery they are mounted in.

Care
Acids in ordinary cardboard, felt and leather will cause silver to tarnish so particular attention should be paid to storing mounted jewellery. Cotton or linen is ideal for packing rings and brooches, but if these are not available use acid-free tissue paper to prevent abrasion. Stringed necklaces should be packed flat to reduce the strain on the string. Labels should be attached with thread as adhesives can harm many gems, amber (see page 79) and pearls (see page 109) in particular.

Before cleaning any jewellery make sure all stones are secure, and always work over a towel or paper in case anything falls off. Do not use any kind of detergents, as these will affect materials such as pearls, opals, ivory, enamel and turquoise. Use a thin brush to clean the small areas of jewellery. Make sure all parts of the jewellery are dry as condensation will form if any parts are still damp.

Let the jewellery air dry and do not use any kind of cloth to dry in case of snagging.

Do not leave in sunlight for prolonged periods as turquoise, topaz and lapis lazuli can change colour or fade, and opals can crack. Amethysts may change colour and garnets and sapphires fracture if exposed to heat. Aquamarines can crack in water and diamonds can scratch other diamonds. Rubies, emeralds, sapphires and topaz can be fractured by sudden knocks.

GLASS

Glass is a broad term that includes glazes, enamels and faience as well as the solid material used for containers, beads and windows etc. Glass itself is not in fact a true solid, but is more accurately described as a super-cooled liquid that has properties of both solids and fluids. This is demonstrated in the 'creep' of old window glass where the panes can appear thicker and rippled at the base as the glass flows very slowly to the bottom.

The composition of glass is largely silica (from sand, quartz or flints), but can vary with the inclusion of other chemicals, which can alter properties such as colour, texture or strength. For example the addition of lead oxide forms lead glass, which can be easily carved or etched. Glass objects can be manufactured by a number of processes – they can be blown free-form, blown into moulds, moulded or floated to make flat planes. Glass can be decorated either in its molten or solid state. It can range from utilitarian to extremely ornate.

Glazed pots have been found dating back to 3000 BC in Mesopotamia. Two thousand years later glass vessels were being hand-blown in Syria using a similar long thin tube to the ones still used today. In the final century BC Roman glassblowers used moulds at the end of glass blowing tubes – this allowed more shapes to be developed and embossed decorations. The Romans also created the first window panes – although they were not the transparent sheets familiar today – Roman window glass was green and virtually opaque, and one surface is usually rough where it was laid flat to dry.

In Britain the use of glass windows left with the Romans, and was replaced with horn sheets. Only in the late medieval period did window glass return – to palaces and in the stained glass of churches.

Identification
Glass is heavy and feels slightly cool to the touch. The colour can vary, but early glass is almost always greenish because of iron impurities.

Soda glass
Soda glass was the main type up to around AD 1000. It can be recognised by a distinctive brown flaky surface.

Potash glass
Materials for soda glass could be difficult and expensive to import, so potash glass became more widely used. Potash can be made by burning wood, or other plant materials, and from sands. Clarity was improved by

adding salt and manganese (in small quantities) but potash glass remains less clear than soda glass.

Lead glass
In 1673 the English glassmaker George Ravenscroft (1618-1681) added lead oxide to potash glass in an attempt to improve the clarity. What resulted was a brilliantly clear, heavy glass that was perfect for etching and carving. The high refractive index also allowed it to be used in precision optics for microscopes and telescopes. It is still used today to make luxury glass 'crystal' items including chandeliers.

Plate glass
Plate glass is a French invention of 1688, originally to provide better mirrors, but that also enabled very large window panes to be manufactured.

Victorian and modern glass
In the late Victorian period and the first quarter of the twentieth century other minerals were added to glass as clarifiers – including manganese dioxide (which turns pink or violet with exposure to the UV in sunlight) and selenium (which can become an amber colour).

Survival
Glass survives in most conditions but is usually damaged and degraded. A dense black film can form on lead glass recovered from anaerobic conditions; however the main problems are caused by devitrification and glass disease.

Devitrification
Any silicaceous material, including glass, flint and obsidian is subject to devitrification, where the surface absorbs moisture and begins to become crystalline. This can cause flaking and crazing, and the surface can appear cloudy or iridescent. All glass is subject to this process, although glass panes are particularly susceptible.

Glass disease
Glass produced before the eighteenth century can suffer from 'glass disease' which is indicated by tiny cracks, pits, flakes and grey or milky scales on the surface. In severe cases the glass may laminate. Glass disease

is caused by the breakdown of the sodium and potassium oxides that were added to the glass during manufacture as a flux to aid fusion. These compounds retain slight amounts of water and this leaches out of the glass, forming droplets on the surface and, in severe cases, the glass can dissolve.

After the eighteenth century glass was produced with a more stable formula and glass disease is unusual in later pieces.

Care

Take care when handling glass items, as with delicate pottery you should never handle glass items by protuberances such as handles, or by fragile areas such as the rim or neck.

Gloves should be worn as iridescent layers can become detached when using bare hands. However, gloves can become slippery so extra care is required.

Never use metal tools to clean glass – only use materials that will not scratch the piece or remove flakes/films on the surface.

Before washing glass ensure it has not been repaired as any adhesive might disintegrate in the water.

Do not immerse soda glass as it will absorb water and begin to dissolve. If the flaking on the glass is not too severe it can be carefully washed with fingers or a sponge and then stored in a water-filled bag, but if it is badly flaked air-dry only. This treatment should also be applied to Roman millaflori glass. Extreme care should be taken with any degraded glass – opinion varies on the best method of both cleaning and storing. However, do not try to clean dirt from iridescent glass.

Only wash glass in tepid water as sudden changes in temperature can crack the piece. Early glass is particularly sensitive to heat and cold. Use a soft brush for washing. Air dry if the piece is stable. Do not dry glass in strong light, near a heat source, or by cooling vents.

Robust, later, glass items (such as some bottles) can be cleaned by immersion in a mixture of water, detergent and water softener with about 25g or raw rice or fine sand added. Gently stirring the mixture should remove much of the dirt. The item can be left to soak for up to 24 hours and then well rinsed to remove the cleaning product residue. Do not clog drains by pouring the rice mixture down the sink.

Glass is often sharp so always clearly state on labels that there is glass in the bag/box to avoid injury and reduce potential for damage. Ensure the item is well supported so it cannot move in the bag or box.

Glass (especially early, degraded or decorated items) is best stored in cool, wet and dark conditions. If in doubt about the best conditions, store the item in a small amount of water.

If not to be stored in water, glass sherds should be separately wrapped in acid-free tissue paper. Remove stoppers from bottles to avoid condensation forming, and do not store glass on metal surfaces which can scratch or stain the piece. The RH of the storage area should not exceed 40 per cent. Always make sure the glass is completely dry before storing as any water present could accelerate decomposition.

GOLD

Gold has probably been *the* precious metal of societies throughout time and occurs in many different circumstances, from jewellery to dentures. It is valued for its malleability and ductility as well as its resistance to acids. It can be found in unexpected places such as in the pigment on some Chinese porcelain, which has to be carefully handled. Gold can also be drawn into the finest wire, the thickness of a human hair, and woven into fabrics. It can be hammered flat into the most delicate of sheets and, used as gold leaf, can be applied to many surfaces from buildings to the end pages of books.

Identification
A shiny yellow metal in its relatively pure form. With the introduction of alloys the colour may change and can vary from white if mixed with silver, to a reddish colour with the inclusion of copper.

Survival
Gold is an almost inert metal and so undergoes minimum corrosion. It is the copper- and/or silver-based gold alloys that easily corrode, resulting in corrosion compounds that leave an enlarged and possibly weakened surface.

Care

If dirty wash in cool water and air-dry. Be aware of composite items. Early gold, particularly that which has been cold hammered and not alloyed, may be fragile.

Gilding should be treated with care as it might lift from the surface particularly if on leather or wood which, if allowed to dry out, may retract leaving the gilding to flake off. Gilding is often soft and so must not be harshly rubbed.

Gold, due to its softness, is often found crushed or bent or becomes brittle with age. No attempt should be made restore these items as it may result in the piece snapping. Any correction of the artefact's state is to deny it it's history.

HORN

Horn, as it is such as malleable material, has been used for myriad types of artefacts. The word lantern comes from lamp-horn as the lantern panes were made from very thin sheets of horn. Horn is almost exclusively taken from cattle; however the horns found at the Sutton Hoo burial are from the now extinct auroch.

Identification

Horn itself is rarely found but its presence can be indicated by other means. The horn sheath (the part used) had to be detached from the bony core – this was usually done by soaking the cores in pits. It is the recovery of these bony cores and pits which indicates horn manufacture.

Survival

Horn, generally, cannot withstand burial beneath the soil for long; it readily delaminates and, being an organic substance, decomposes quickly. Therefore, archaeological finds are few, and those that have been unearthed tend to be of the later rather than the earlier periods.

Care

If it is recovered keep wet and treat carefully as horn will laminate quickly. Do not use metal tools as the horn is very soft and may be marked. Store in an RH of 45–50 per cent and keep away from heat and light.

IRON

Iron has been used extensively throughout history from around 1000 BC. Water and air cause oxidation (rust) which, if not arrested, will continue until the whole item is reduced to powder. This is the reason why so few iron items are found in relation to the number made. In antiquity, iron was hammered to form joins and these easy to see in an x-ray. Cast iron was not used until medieval times in Europe.

Identification
Often a brown 'rust' coloured item can be heavily concreted or have thin areas where corrosion is present – it can be difficult to tell if iron is present. If in doubt use a magnet, however, very old or deeply corroded iron may have a weak response so do not dismiss it if there is little response from the magnet.

Survival
When corroded different effects can be seen:
• Grit and small stone concretion – often from aerated soils
• White to light grey coating – recovered from chalk soils.
• Black even texture (occasionally with blue patches) – from anaerobic or waterlogged conditions.
• Bright orange protuberances and light in weight – from well aerated soils.
• Orange-brown on outermost layer – from aerobic soils. Can be very thick and obscure shape of original.
• Blue – from phosphate soils.

Iron does not survive well in sea water where the salt in the water accelerated oxidation.

Care
In general, do not get iron items wet – leave to air dry and brush gently to remove surface dirt. Do not allow an item to dry too quickly (such as leaving it next to a heater) because as it dries it may begin to break up. If this does happen keep any pieces with the artefact. Some sturdy iron objects such as horseshoes and nails can be washed and left to air dry.

Be aware that some iron objects may have textile or organic evidence adhering or attached to them (such as an ivory handle on a knife).

All iron should be placed in an airtight plastic box, if necessary supported with acid-free tissue paper and with silica gel added. A humidity strip should be in the box. If no box is available then use a polythene bag with silica gel inside and close securely.

If there is a strong response from a magnet in one area of a piece and weak in another, cleaning should progress with extreme care as the item may break in two. A good example of this is a pair of scissors where the loops may be thinner than the handles. Any projections on the item may also be thinner.

Comparing the weight to the size can often give an indication of how much of the original item is left as a heavy item will have less oxidised material than a lighter one of the same size.

IVORY

True ivory comes from African and Indian elephants, mammoths and mastodons. The term is often expanded to include materials from other mammals such as the hippopotamus, walrus and narwhal. Ivory has been used from early times, often as a luxury material to replace bone.

Identification

Ivory resembles bone and it can be difficult to tell them apart. Indications to look for are fine lines and the absence of dots that typify bone. Some bone will also have spongy areas that are not found in ivory. Ivory is slightly heavier and softer than bone and as it ages it becomes whiter whereas bone yellows.

Fossilised
mammoth ivory
showing growth
lines

Survival

In dry conditions ivory can become brittle and pieces may break up. Ivory does not survive well in waterlogged conditions where it can become spongy and delicate. Ivory can also fossilise as the bony material is replaced by mineral salts and silica.

Ivory can be damaged or destroyed by sea water or a salty atmosphere – the salts absorbed can crystallise and cause flaking of the surface. Heat and damp will also damage ivory and immersion in water will cause decomposition.

Care

Maintain the piece according to the conditions it is recovered from. Dry wet ivory slowly or the piece can split along joins. However, it is probably best to keep the piece wet until a conservator can deal with it.

Do not allow dry ivory to become wet as it will laminate – clean only with a brush or puffer brush and take care not to flake or scratch the surface.

If the ivory has been exposed to salty conditions it must be stabilised by rinsing in water to remove the salts. Tap water can be used to remove the salts initially, followed by deionised water for final rinsing.

Consolidating ivory is difficult, but can be done by soaking in permeable soluble nylon, and then drying immediately in ether or alcohol. Ivory should be stored at an RH of 45-50 per cent.

JADE

Jade is a hardstone and comes in two types – a sodium–aluminium silicate called jadeite and a silicate of calcium and magnesium called nephrite. Green jade stone axes from the Neolithic have been found in Spain, Portugal, Western Germany, Britain and France (particularly tombs in Brittany). One of the best known examples is the 'Canterbury Axe' on display in the British Museum. Roughly 23cm long with an elongated triangular form it is distinguished from other jade axes which are typically symmetrical with a pointed butt and show little evidence of use. Perhaps the most familiar form of jade is that extensively used by Chinese for small carvings. Too hard to be cut with tools it has to be ground by abrasives in oily or wet conditions.

Identification

Jadeite is 7 on the Mohs scale whilst nephrite is 6.5. They are too hard to be scratched by metal tools and both have a range of colours from white, brown, mauve, blue, yellow, red, grey and black although the apple-green colour is usually unique to jadeite. They are cool to the touch.

Survival

Jadeite and nephrite survive well but when buried for a long time, both the colour and the quality of the surface can change.

Care

As hardstones they can be easily cleaned. As they are hard enough to scratch glass they should not be stored with other softer materials.

JET

Jet is a form of fossilised wood that can be carved and polished to gemstone quality. Although jet was mainly used for jewellery it can also be found as handles, paper knives, paper weights and ornaments.

Jet is found or mined at a number of locations, including France and Spain – but perhaps the most famous UK source are the 170 million-year-old beds at Whitby in Yorkshire, which produce two types: soft (from the upper beds - Mohs 2); and hard (from the lower beds - Mohs 3). Whitby remains a small centre of production, but the main sources have been exhausted and much of the jet comes from pebbles washed up on the beach.

Jet has been used since the Neolithic period but its hardness made it difficult to work until the introduction of stronger tools in the Bronze Age, when it was used mainly for beads, v-shaped perforated buttons and conical studs. A necklace of over 100 beads was found at Kill y Kiaran, Scotland, and can now be seen at the National Museums of Scotland, Edinburgh. Bronze Age beads were often long rather than round (as they are easier to hold when carving).

Iron Age finds are rare and the use of jet declined towards the end of the Roman occupation. The Vikings and Saxons used it intermittently – it was exported from Viking York (Jorvic) to Scandinavia.

In the eighteenth century machines were introduced that enabled carved jet to be produced more cheaply. There was a boom in jet jewellery following the death of Prince Albert when mourning jewellery became very fashionable, but it was also common to use cheaper materials, such as vulcanite and glass. The mood of the nation lightened by around 1880 and there was a slump in the demand for jet, but it is still used for jewellery today as it is the only truly black stone that is relatively inexpensive and comparatively easy to work.

Identification
Unpolished jet is a dull greyish stone that only appears black when polished or broken. Some pieces may show evidence of wood grain or tree rings. It is light in weight and warm to the touch and, like coal, it will burn, giving off a greenish flame. Hard, strong tools are needed to carve jet, but it will break easily on impact, with conchoidal fracture lines. Carving jet produces a distinctive pungent odour. Scratching raw jet may leave brownish marks.

Like amber, jet can become statically charged when rubbed, picking up dust and lint. Also like amber it can be found on beaches, washed up by the sea.

Survival
Jet survives in most soil conditions but particularly well in waterlogged sites.

Care
Take care when washing dry jet as it can shatter in hot water and as it dries out, so air-dry away from any heat sources. As an alternative to washing, dry jet can be cleaned by rubbing gently with fresh breadcrumbs. Jet can also be easily scratched, so keep away from sharp or hard objects and pack separately using a foam backing. Wet jet should be kept wet. Composite items can be quite delicate.

LEAD

Lead is a metal that corrodes very rapidly so evidence of its use in prehistory is probably lost. It is a soft grey/white, easily malleable metal which tarnishes readily. It has a melting point of 327°C so can be heated with a domestic fire. Lead items have been recovered from the Bronze

Age where it was used for weights, spindle whorls and net sinkers as well as moulds to cast socketed axes. The use of lead did not become popular until the Roman period when it would be used for, amongst other things, coffins, pipes and roofing.

Identification
Lead is a heavy grey/white metal often found badly corroded where it is reduced to powdery carbonates that cannot even be excavated. When this happens mark on the sheet the presence of lead.

Survival
Lead does not survive well in acidic soils or waterlogged conditions. Corrosion effects are similar to that of tin and pewter. Severe corrosion will reduce the lead to a friable surface with light grey patches and dark grey warts. The most common corroded appearance is a white to grey surface coating, often underneath a fine light brown soil/corrosion mixture.

Objects made with a large content of lead are commonly distorted when recovered because of the softness of the metal.

Care
Do not wash and if recovered wet allow slow drying. If recovered dry gently brush off the worst of the corrosion.

Lead is particularly susceptible to attack by organic acids found in wood, paper products, paint, varnishes and fabrics. Therefore do not store in anything other than acid-free materials or in polythene bags, making sure they are well ventilated. Examine regularly for white powdery spots which may indicate contamination.

Lead is very vulnerable as it bends easily. Do not attempt to restore the shape as it will be likely to snap. Use no metal tools on lead and do not store with anything which can scratch it.

LEATHER

Leather is the prepared skin of animals, commonly domestic, but many expensive items are made from exotic species.

Leather has been used throughout history for a range of purposes including clothes, shoes, armour, and containers of many kinds. The

Chinese used leather coins from the second century BC, as did other cultures including the Romans (the word pecuniary comes from the Latin *pecos*, meaning hide), the practice continued up to the twentieth century in Germany. Leather was also used to make parchment and vellum, and for book bindings.

By the medieval age most towns had a tannery, often placed well away from the town centre because producing leather is a very smelly operation. Many towns have streets with names such as Leather Lane, Tanner Street or Bark Street, where the tanneries operated, usually close to the river or another water source.

Leather Production
Preparation

Before tanning hides must be cleaned of hair, fat and muscle tissue, which is usually scraped off. Skin varies in thickness according to the type and age of the source animal. Thick skins were often split through the middle layer to produce two layers – the outer side producing 'grain' leather (named after the tough collagen fibre layer – 'corium' – that gives it strength and durability); the inner layer for suede.

Young animals, like calves and baby goats have much thinner skin and this is used to produce the finest leathers, as they are soft, flexible (and often very expensive). Arabian 'morocco' leather, from goatskin, was highly prized in medieval times and is still considered to be the benchmark for quality.

Hides can still be used without tanning, as 'rawhide' which when soaked has the useful property of shrinking and setting hard. It has been used as a binding material from the earliest times.

Tanning

The hides of dead animals will rot unless they are preserved by tanning to convert them into leather, a process which also makes the hide more workable. The process requires the treatment of the hide with tannins – chemicals that are found in a variety of natural sources including ground bark and alum. Tanned leather over 7000 years old has been found, but it is not known when the process first started. Up to the Industrial Revolution hides were soaked in pits filled with tannins. This process can be very slow, so tanneries had a number of pits where hides could soak for up to two years.

Chemical tanning was introduced in the 1880s along with new machinery that made mass-production possible.

Other treatments

After tanning, leather is usually hung for several days and then shaved to achieve a consistent thickness.

Natural leather comes in a range of colours that depend on the hide used and the treatment received, but it is common for leather to be dyed. Dyes can be used to create leather of virtually any colour. Leather can also be decorated by painting and tooling – thick leather is often carved or punched with awls into sometimes complex patterns and pictures; and it can be stamped to make repetitive designs. Pieces of leather can be sewn together, although it is generally too tough for early bone and metal needles. Rivets, often made from copper, were also used to join leather, and for decoration.

Softening of leather can be done by a number of mechanical and chemical means, ranging from chewing, rolling, stretching and oiling. Where leather was to be used for gloves and other items that needed to be very soft and flexible, tanners would add oils to the tanning pits.

Identification

The follicles and sweat glands of animal skin give leather distinctive patterns that can be used to identify the animal used. As tanners would split hides the thickness of a piece of leather is not a good indicator of the type of hide.

Survival

Leather is commonly found in excavations, most often in waterlogged sites such as marshes, wells and ditches, but its condition will depend on a number of factors including the way it was tanned and the type of hide used. Damage can occur in a number of ways (and combinations):

- Very dry leather can be shrunk, cracked, broken and very brittle.
- Light exposure can fade the material and also cause cracking and flaking.
- Wet conditions will cause the leather to rot from mould and bacterial activity. Rotting leather has a distinctive unpleasant smell and can look stained and distorted. The leather will be soft and may tear easily.
- Leather can provide a good food source for insects and other animals and holes can indicate infestation.

- Metal associated with the leather (buckles, rivets, etc.) can corrode, staining and softening the material. The degree of damage is related to the metal used.
- If leather has been folded or rested on an edge, splitting and cracking can occur.
- Cleaning materials and leather dressings can cause great damage. Leather soaps, oils and lubricants often contain harsh alkaline chemicals which can break down the tanning of the leather and result in oxidation, rotting and distortion of the item.

Care

Leather can be difficult to process and conserve, both because of the variety of conditions it can be found in and the fact that it is so often a component of a more complex artefact. The recommended methods are constantly changing as more research is done.

Much recovered leather is part of a composite item and wherever possible any metal components should be removed. If this is not possible, for example with shoes or animal harnesses, the metal should be cleaned to avoid corrosion damaging the leather. For complex items, where layers of leather have been used in construction, only the surface soil should be removed – conservators can dismantle the piece in the laboratory where the relationship of the individual components can be better recorded.

Before processing, take measurements of the leather as wetting or drying can alter the size. Always have clean hands when handling leather and never use tools that may leave a mark.

Do not use commercial cleaning soaps or oils – they may improve appearance but they cannot easily be removed and may cause changes in the material. It is essential that any process used can be reversed. As stated in the American Institute for Conservation of Historic and Artistic Works (AIC) Code of Ethics – the conservator:

> should avoid the use of materials which may become so intractable that their future removal could endanger the physical safety of the object. They also should avoid the use of techniques, the results of which cannot be undone if that should become desirable.

Wet leather should be washed in tepid water using fingers or a soft sponge. Use enough water to cover the piece. Do not try to remove old stains as these can provide important information about the piece. Dry in air, away from heat and strong light.

Leather recovered wet should be stored wet to avoid drying and cracking and then passed to conservators for processing. Seal in two bags and place in airtight boxes. Before sealing the bags remove as much air as possible, and change the storage water often to avoid rotting from bacterial action and drying out. Do not use fungicides or any other chemical in the water as these can interfere with carbon dating and leave deposits on the item. Ensure labels are marked with waterproof ink. Store away from heat, and in the dark if possible – black bin bags can be used to keep light from fading the items.

If leather is recovered dry it should be gently brushed clean or vacuumed. Use a soft brush to avoid marking the piece (recommended by the Canadian Conservation Institute (1992)).

Dry leather will be very susceptible to humidity which can cause rot. If the leather must be stored for any length of time the RH must not exceed 55 per cent (mould starts to grow above 65 per cent) and should be kept as stable as possible (Calnan 1991).

The temperature should be between 18-22°C. Do not seal in bags as this can encourage condensation, and keep away from light.

Do not fold materials or place on their edge – add supports to the storage to prevent the leather cracking and distorting. For shoes an internal support should be used in addition to external to maintain the shape. Dust can also be a problem, as it acts as an abrasive and can be difficult to remove from the grain and any decorations. Leather should be stored under a cover to minimise dust collection.

MARBLE

Marble is a re-crystallised (metamorphosed) limestone and has been used in building throughout the world from the earliest times.

Identification
Marble is a soft stone, easily carved and takes a high polish. The coloured streaks in marble are impurities, such as iron oxides, that entered gaps in the stone staining it in a wide variety of colours and shapes.

Survival

Marble will not survive well in waterlogged conditions as it is a porous stone. It can also be stained easily.

Care

Marble scratches easily so do not scrape with any kind of metal tool. As it is porous it can be stained by straw or wood or newspaper. Flawed pieces will give a dull thud when tapped gently as opposed to the clear ring of an unflawed block.

METALS

Certain metal items such as coins and other items of specific interest should be taken both at the end of the morning session and the end of the day to the finds hut for collection by the processor. On exposure to air, any existing corrosion in recovered metals can be accelerated so metals need to be dried out as soon as possible. In the finds hut there should be Tupperware or plastic food storage boxes for metals and coins. These boxes will include sachets of silica gel intended to absorb the moisture from the metals and it is important that, after placing metal items in the box, that the lid is securely replaced. If the lid is not replaced securely the silica gel will become saturated from moisture in the air and will cease to work. Usually there is a large notice to this effect plastered on top of the box to remind diggers.

MOTHER-OF-PEARL

Also known as nacre, mother-of-pearl is the build-up of layers forming the lining of the shell of a number of species of fresh- and saltwater molluscs, chiefly the oyster and nautilus. It is used for inlaying (down to half a millimetre) and a large number of small decorative items. The surface can be etched, carved or incised. Mother-of-pearl has a conformity that means large amounts of it can be used without have to select finer quality items. Small offcuts were used for button making and, at the beginning of the nineteenth century, Birmingham became a leading centre for button manufacture. By 1879 French imports were flooding in, and the United States also become a competitor. Eventually competition forced the Birmingham industry to cease and tons of shell was dumped. However, only a few years later it became so popular again that people were digging up their back gardens trying to find the hoards of shell.

Identification

Mother-of-pearl is prismatic, reflecting light back to the eye. It is composed of the same material as pearls, calcium carbonate, but of course pearls are much rarer. The colour of mother-of-pearl varies according to the sea the shell developed in.

Survival

Mother-of-pearl survives well in waterlogged conditions but not in acidic soils.

Care

Mother-of-pearl is a soft material, 3-4 on the Mohs scale. It dissolves easily in acids so keep all cleaning solutions away from it.

Long exposure to light will cause it to dull and so mother-of-pearl should be kept covered or in low light environments. Mother-of-pearl is porous and will absorb water so if recovered dry do not get wet, but if recovered wet keep wet.

ORGANICS

When organic items are removed from damp soil keep them wet as if allowed to dry quickly, they will crack and degrade. If organic objects are not removed to the finds processor then monitor them and, if necessary, keep a plant spray nearby to regularly spray the item.

PEARL

A pearl is the concretion of calcium carbonate material that fresh- and saltwater molluscs produces to encapsulate a foreign body within its shell. The pearl most often used is from the oyster.

There are three types of commercially available pearls: true, blister and cultured. Natural or true pearls have often come at a high price as pearl divers have died when diving to recover them from wild oysters. Blister pearls form naturally on the inside of the shell. Cultured pearls are cultivated by introducing a foreign object to induce the oyster to produce a pearl. There are also artificial pearls made by injecting hollow glass with a mixture of the scales of freshwater fish and ammonia which coats the inside of the hollow glass.

Identification
The pearl is built up in a series of thin layers and it is this layering which is responsible for the iridescent sheen. Pearls come in many shapes: åspherical, drop- or pear-shaped, *bouton* (dome-shaped) or *baroque* (irregular shape) and many different colours such as white, yellow, rose, blue, grey and the rare black. Draw a real pearl across the teeth and it will feel rough.

Survival
Pearls will survive in neutral soils but not in acidic.

Care
No cleaning agents should be used on pearls as they are dissolved even by the weakest of acids.

PEWTER

Pewter is an alloy of tin mixed with a number of other metals, including lead (used by the Romans in a wide range of percentages), antimony (introduced in the seventeenth century), bismuth and copper. The make-up of the alloy has varied – due to its toxicity lead is not included in modern pewter, which is now composed of: 94 per cent tin, 4 per cent antimony, 2 per cent copper or bismuth. (British Standards Authority 1969). Britannia metal is considered by some to be a form of pewter as it is primarily an alloy of tin, but this is controversial.

The inclusion of other metals makes pewter harder and more malleable than tin, which is quite brittle and splits easily when hammered. The alloy becomes soft as it is worked so it does not have to be heated.

Pewter was used for a wide range of tableware – replacing the use of horn, wood and pottery for cups and plates. It was also used for organ pipes. The moulds used were expensive to produce so there are a number of very traditional shapes. The introduction of more attractive materials such as porcelain and glass reduced the widespread use of pewter.

Identification

Pewter is heavy and has a variety of colours depending on the metals used in the alloy. Often greyish/silver, it can also be nearly white or very dark grey. Colour can also come from its surroundings – if stored in a smoky environment, such as a kitchen, it can take on a brownish tinge.

Marks

The makers of pewter items would often add a mark or 'touch' – usually a cartouche of the maker's initials and sometimes a device. In 1603 all pewter was obliged to carry a maker's mark.

In the late seventeenth century the marks began to bear the full name of the manufacturer along with a town and quality mark.

Town marks vary – they can be the coat of arms, device or seal; or simply the name or initials of the town. London pewter bears the full city name, but as it was appreciated for its quality some makers in other towns also stamped their wares with the name of the capital – so provenance may not be proven simply by a London mark.

The original quality mark was the Tudor rose and crown which was used to indicate that the item was destined for export. The mark soon became known as a mark of quality and so from 1543 onwards the rose mark became obligatory.

Dates were also added, although they do not always indicate the date of manufacture but the date the maker joined their guild. Dates are also shown as the establishment of the family, factory or company.

Copying silver marks was common in the early seventeenth century, despite the attempts of the Goldsmiths Company to prevent it. So marks such as lions (passant and rampant), leopard's heads, anchors and thistles can be found.

In the eighteenth century pewter makers were at pains to emphasise the quality of their wares and used terms such as 'superfine hard metal' in addition to other marks to show that a low lead content had been used.

Before the introduction of imperial standards in 1826 the marks included the monarchs initial beneath a crown (such as AR for Queen Anne). When the standards were put in place the monarch's initials and number was used – GIV, VR etc – occasionally with the word 'imperial' or borough or county stamps. Marks can be seen in Peal (1971).

Survival
Pewter can be damaged by damp and cold as, with such a high tin content, it is subject to 'tin pest'.

Care
Do not wash dry pewter items unless absolutely necessary (use warm water) – it is better to clean with a soft brush. Air-dry wet items. Pack in a polythene bag inside a dry (preferably transparent) box containing silica gel, artsorb and a humidifier strip. Place the item on a bed of acid-free tissue paper if fragile. Store small items on their own.

Do not store small finds with bulk finds but always on their own and, if necessary in a clear plastic box.

PLASTER

Plaster is a mortar covered with a lime-wash layer that may or may not be decorated. If a site yields a large amount of plain plaster then there may be a policy to keep only any decorated pieces found. Painted wall plaster (PWP) is common on many Roman sites and is generally an indication of affluent living.

Identification
The reverse side of PWP is usually an uneven conglomerate of plaster which is greyish/whitish in colour. The front side will be a smooth white surface if plain, coloured or decorated if painted.

Survival
Poor in waterlogged areas as it will simply disintegrate. In dry areas recovery is variable.

Care

Never get plaster wet as it will disintegrate. If recovered damp do not rub at the surface to clean, dab gently with a sponge. If the dirt does not come off, leave any further processing for a conservator.

If recovered damp make sure it is completely dry before packing, as any condensation will rot the plaster. Do not place too close to a heater as the pieces could dry out too quickly and fragment. Ensure that plaster is dried face upwards as if dried face down the paint could stick to the paper and become removed. Do not touch painted surfaces with the fingers as grease may be transferred.

POTTERY

Notes of the recovery of pottery have been covered previously.

Identification

Pottery can be divided into four main categories: earthenware (also called coarseware), stoneware, porcelain and bone china.

EARTHENWARE

Identification

Prehistoric pottery, and much pottery up to medieval times, will be quite coarse in its makeup. This coarseware will be heavily tempered with other materials such as burnt and plain flint and shell. The colour will depend on the clays used, the mineral inclusions and the firing conditions, but mainly it is white, buff, brown, red and grey. Coarseware does not allow light to pass through it and is heavy in comparison to modern earthenware and porcelains.

Handmade pottery is usually coil built, using long sausage-like coils which are circled one on top of another to build up the body. Look for the irregular circular lines usually on the inside of the vessel that indicate a coil pot.

By the first century BC wheel-made pottery was being imported from the Roman world. Like coil-built wares, wheel-made pottery will have circular lines on the interior. However, unlike handmade pottery these

Coil lines   Wheel lines

will be evenly spaced and the lines straighter. By the fifth century the art of wheel-made pottery had been lost (or was perhaps not needed) and pottery was once again handmade in similar forms to that of the pre-Roman era. There is therefore a similarity between pottery of the Iron Age and Saxon age, so taken care when dating coarseware.

Cleaning

All earthenware or earthenware based pottery should be washed with care. The older the earthenware the more friable it will be and as a general rule prehistoric pottery should not be washed. All earthenware is non-porous and so subject to disintegration when placed in water, so it should never be immersed.

Prehistoric pottery, such as Neolithic, was often burnished during manufacture – that is, rubbed with a stone or hard object in order to close the pores thereby making it a little more waterproof. A careful watch needs to be made for this as the burnishing can flake and therefore be removed with vigorous washing.

Often pottery temper will included plants, hay, straw, flint, etc and environmental information can be gained about the plants of the time. Burnt flint in itself can be very friable and if used as a temper in pottery it can quickly disintegrate if washed too forcefully.

Friable pot should be cleaned with either a sponge or gently with the fingers, never with a brush as this will leave scratch marks on the surface thereby obliterating diagnostic features such as coil or wheel lines and decoration. If it is apparent the pot is too friable to be washed then leave it to dry and if possible brush it lightly with a camera lens brush or a face powder brush. If the dirt does not dislodge easily leave it – pottery specialists would rather have complete but dirty pieces than lots of small unidentifiable fragments.

Residues may also be included inside a pot, so take care when cleaning the base of the interior.

A special word about amphorae

It can be difficult to identify Roman amphora as often these are mistaken for Roman building material. Amphorae are usually very thick walled vessels and similar in thickness to Roman bricks – they can also be the same colour, a pale yellow. To differentiate between the two you should look for the handmade coil lines on the interior side of the piece. Amphorae may also show a slight curve from the rounded nature of the vessel, whereas building material rarely curves.

Some amphorae have painted inscriptions and these should be considered when washing, although spotting these can be difficult when bulk washing, particularly when using a power spray.

GLAZES

In order to make earthenware, non-porous glazes were added providing a smooth, translucent or opaque (coloured or white) surface. Glazes were not common before the late twelfth century and are divided into two categories:

LEAD GLAZE

Identification

This is a transparent glassy glaze, found on pottery from the second century AD to the eighteenth century, when Wedgwood used it on his Creamware. Characteristic signs are pinholes and crazing, or a series of fine lines or cracks across the piece, which results from the glaze not bonding with the body completely. The glaze can chip easily and most pieces have not escaped unscathed.

TIN PLATE

Identification

Ceramics with tin glazes appear from the fifteenth century onwards and come under various names in various parts of the world such as maiolica (Italy from the fifteenth century), majolica (England from the nineteenth century), Delft (Dutch from the sixteenth century), delft (English from seventeenth century. Note the small d for English and capital D for Dutch) or faience (France and Germany).

Tin ware has an opaque white finish influenced by the desire of the Europeans to imitate Chinese porcelain. It is a soft, easily damaged glaze and therefore not suited to much daily use. It is easily marked by acidic fruit and cannot stand hot water (which is the origin of putting milk into teacups before adding the tea). It looks like egg shell and will chip and crack easily, and like lead glaze early pieces rarely survive intact.

Cleaning

With all glazed earthenware check for chips or cracks before washing. If they are present the water can enter the non-porous areas. This is particularly true of the foot rim, which is often left unglazed to allow the piece to stand and dry. Watch also for copper and iron rivets, for if a piece is valuable it may have been repaired. If the copper or iron becomes wet and is not dried properly it may stain the piece.

If the piece is stable then wash according to its state with either a sponge or fingers. A toothbrush or nail brush may be used, but only if the piece is stable as with Creamware. Many glazed earthenware pieces will have been decorated with pictures or designs, so care must be taken not to accidentally remove the design if the glaze is badly cracked. Delphware may lose its glaze if washed too vigorously.

The fabric of the pot can sometimes be very powdery so do not wash. Some glazes can be affected by soluble salt action and will deposit white salty blobs. These pieces should be stored wet and taken to a conservation lab, as if allowed to dry out the salt particles will cause the glaze to break up (see page 67).

STONEWARE

Identification

Stoneware is an impervious, solid and durable ceramic developed in Germany at the end of the fourteenth century. Most familiar stonewares are brown (coloured by the iron inclusions) such as the bellamine jugs, or the later domestic ceramics made of durable stoneware such as the ginger beer bottle or ink wells of the Victorian era. However, there is white stoneware (1740s onwards), bright blue German ware such as Westerwald (1587 onwards) and other colours from dark brown to red, grey, or buff coloured. Stoneware can be thinly potted and is sometimes mistaken for porcelain. The texture can range from rough (with a look similar to orange peel) to smooth.

Much sewer and drainage piping was (and still is) made from stoneware due to its durability. Many inexperienced archaeologists send up pieces of water pipe thinking it stoneware pottery. It is important to remember that stoneware pipes can be very thick, and so a thick piece of supposed pot will probably be a drainage pipe.

Cleaning

As the brown type of stoneware is so hard and durable it can be washed with either a toothbrush or nail brush, or power sprayed and left to air-dry. More care needs to be taken with the thinner types and although these can be washed with brushes, there is a need to be careful to avoid breakages.

PORCELAIN

Identification

Porcelain was a Chinese invention (206 BC-AD 220) much admired in Europe which sparked off a race to imitate it, resulting in the development of tin glazed pottery. The first real European porcelain was developed at Meissen, Germany in 1709. The term porcelain is an umbrella name for all translucent paste bodies. There are two forms of European porcelain, hard-paste, or 'true' porcelain (as it comes closest to Chinese porcelain) and soft-paste porcelain which was in use until hard-paste was developed.

Porcelain will ring with a metallic sound when flicked with the fingernails, and will sound similar to glass when struck. If the piece appears to be porcelain but emits a dull sound, it may be that the piece has been repaired. If held up to the light and a hand placed behind the piece a shadowy silhouette of the hand should be seen through the translucent body. It is extremely tough and can withstand boiling water and, because it is the hardest ceramic porcelain, is often used for electrical insulators and laboratory equipment. It is characterised by a pure whiteness and although it looks delicate it is hard and cold looking. Porcelain is usually glazed and often has transfer decoration (first used in 1750).

Cleaning
As it is relatively robust porcelain can be cleaned with brushes and power sprayed, but obviously care is needed as it can be brittle and prone to chipping. Also avoid scrubbing gilded or decorated areas.

BONE CHINA

Identification
Often bone china is placed in the porcelain category as it is made with hard-paste porcelain ingredients, but these only account for 50 per cent of its composition. The other half of the ingredients is calcined bone ash (usually ox bone, roasted or partially fused in the kiln then ground to a powder). However, it can also be placed in the soft-paste porcelain category as it is fired at a lower temperature than hard-paste.

Bone China was created *c.*1794 by Spode and by 1918 all major British companies were making it. It is an almost purely British ceramic.

The bone ash makes the body an ivory white in colour and more translucent than porcelain. Whilst it is not quite as durable as hard-paste porcelain, it is more durable than soft-paste porcelain. Maker's marks that include the words 'bone china' are twentieth-century in date.

Cleaning
As with porcelain, if it is relatively robust, bone china can be cleaned with brushes and power sprayed, but care is needed as it can be brittle and prone to chipping. Also avoid scrubbing gilded or decorated areas. Surface details may not always be on the outside, decorations can occur inside the

pot as well. If lids are present store the pieces with the lids off but kept to one side so they do not become orphaned. Do not tape down the lids to the objects as, if left for a long time, the tape may damage the piece.

SHELL

Snail and oyster shell are not collected on site unless specifically required. Oyster and snail shells are only collected as part of an environmental sample where they occur in large numbers. If large deposits are found then a sampling policy will be put into place. Single oyster shells should not be collected, as it was a common food throughout most of history and single or a handful of examples will yield no information unless they have been worked in some way (such as pierced). Shells on site fall into four categories:

- those brought from the sea shore as food and discarded locally often as a midden (a waste heap). These shells can provide information about diet and travel.
- those that act as containers, spoons and tools.
- those utilised for a specific purpose such as the Mediterranean *murex* from which the Romans extracted a purple dye. This practice was so expensive that only emperors were allowed to wear purple clothes.
- those used as charms, jewellery (and even trumpets). Small shells were used as beads and pendants by the first anatomically modern humans, and have been in constant use ever since.
- Carved shells – again these have been produced since pre-history but by 1852 the French had started mass-producing shell carvings, and by the late nineteenth century shell carving was so popular that the British Museum refused to take any more. The Victoria & Albert Museum (just starting its collection at this time), did take the more ornate examples.

Identification

Nautilus shell
The nautilus is found in the Pacific and Indian oceans. The shell has a chambered structure and has a highly colourful yellow and orange

exterior with iridescent nacre inside. The exterior of the shell is soft enough to carve with a penknife and it was often formed into intricate designs. The most common decoration method was to engrave the shell and fill in lines with coal mixed with wax and oil (similar to scrimshaw) before mounting. However, the shell is very thin and carving it has been compared to cutting newspaper. It is also very weak and prone to break. Nautilus shells began to appear in the nineteenth century but by the Victorian times they had declined in popularity.

Cameo

Before the term was expanded to include carved gems, it applied to the carving of shells. The requisite characteristics of a cameo shell is that it must have at least a two-colour structure to achieve the contrast and included shells such as helmet shells, cowries and conches. Either the whole shell was carved or broken up to make smaller items such as brooches or shirt studs.

Cowry

The cowry has a long history. As the bottom of shell was supposed to resemble a woman's sexual parts the shell became associated with Venus, the goddess of love. They are often found in Roman burials and medieval artists cut away the surface to decorate. Cowry shells have a spotted exterior, a white middle and a base colour, the most common of which is purple. The outside shell is fairly soft and can wear away and break easily.

Conches

Conches were often used for cameo and the queen conch was also valued for its meat. It may also contain a pink pearl.

Dentalium shells

So named because it resembles an elephant tusk, there are about 350 species in ocean waters. The shell is open at both ends so it can be threaded and in North American societies they were used as money by several tribes.

Survival

Shells have variable survival – they will not survive in acidic soils but survive well in waterlogged conditions.

Care
Wash in tepid water with a soft brush and air-dry. Be aware of composite items, and handle all shells with care as they are often very fragile.

SILVER

Identification
Silver is a white metal which can be polished to a high shine. It is hard but easily scratched.

Silver is usually found tarnished, covered in either a black silver chloride layer (especially in salt-rich air) or a purplish silver sulphide layer that can appear waxy.

Coins are rarely found without considerable corrosion, due to the copper used in manufacture.

Survival
As a metal silver does not survive well in acidic soils. It is also unusual to recover silver from salt water.

Silver can be lightly tarnished or completely corroded – the silver compounds that form the tarnish are not generally strong and finds can be very fragile. If there is a source of sulphur production nearby, silver will tarnish very rapidly.

Care
If silver is found dry do not wash or wet it – brush the dirt gently away with a soft brush to avoid scratching. Air dry wet items.

Moisture and humidity will degrade silver so items should be carefully packed in a polythene bag inside a dry (preferably transparent) box – on acid-free tissue paper if delicate. Use silica gel or Artsorb to protect the piece and place a humidifier strip inside the box so that the humidity can be monitored. Store small pieces on their own.

Silver in good condition with little tarnishing can be cleaned – always use a good quality polish and clean the item slowly and carefully to avoid thinning the metal. Traces of polish should be removed with warm water. Silver gilt can be cleaned with warm water only.

STEEL

Steel is made by heating iron to 900°c in a charcoal fire so there is a slow penetration of the carbon into the iron. Until the nineteenth century steel was hard to make and its use was restricted to a thin piece on the blade of cutting tools, as it was cheaper than making the whole blade of steel. Steel taints the taste of food, a problem overcome only from the introduction of 'stainless' steel in 1856.

Identification
Steel looks similar to iron but will have a lighter ring to it if tapped *very* gently.

Survival
Steel is less susceptible to rust than iron and survives well.

Care
Treat the same as iron (see page 98).

STONE

Europe has a great variety of rocks but not every rock can be utilised. Not only does it have to be suitable to be worked but it must also have good weathering properties. Building materials are usually taken from local stones due to the high cost of transporting them. Only a few types of stone were used in antiquity. Of these, flint, obsidian, soapstone, limestone, marble, alabaster and serpentine are the most important.

Identification

Igneous rocks
Igneous rocks are formed by the solidification of molten rock or magma. They are very durable and resistant to water and chemicals. Classification is based on two characteristics – chemistry and grain size. When magma cools slowly, individual crystals develop and so rocks are coarse-grained. When magma cools quickly, as is the case when it reaches the surface, there is poor crystal growth and the rock is said to be fine-grained.

Granite

Granite is a coarse-grained rock and the crystals can be seen with the naked eye. It is the most widely used igneous rock for building purposes and the colours range from pink to white.

South-west England and Scotland are important granite producing areas. Some granites, such as those from Aberdeen, are characterised by having all the minerals of the same grain size and so present a uniform appearance. In other granites, such as those from Shap Fell, Devon and Cornwall, the feldspar crystals are much larger than other minerals, giving a less uniform appearance.

Basalt

Basalt is a fine-grained rock with probably the most famous outcrop at Giant's Causeway in Northern Ireland. It is often quarried for road stone as it is extremely hardwearing.

Sedimentary rocks

Sedimentary rocks are those of a secondary origin. They are made from sediments of other rocks, consolidated by pressure. Sedimentary rocks are usually named after their main constituents, so a rock rich in calcium carbonate is known as limestone. Those consisting mainly of sand are sandstones. Limestone and sandstone are the principle sedimentary rocks used in building.

Chalk

Chalk is found extensively in the southern and eastern parts of England where it can be seen exposed in places such as the White Cliffs of Dover and Beachy Head. It consists mainly of calcium carbonate although often fossils can be found. It is usually white, easily quarried, easy to carve, but does not weather well. Where it is used for building it is often combined with brick or harder limestone at the corners.

Limestone

Limestone is formed from the hard remains of living organisms such as shells, corals and other marine life. Calcium carbonate is usually the main constituent chemically, but limestone can also be made from magnesium carbonate such as those found in Yorkshire. Limestone is widely used in building as it is durable, attractive and easily worked. In Britain a wide choice is available, with individual properties and colouring caused by staining from other materials such as iron.

Some well known ones are the carboniferous limestone of the Pennines which are hard, blue-grey and crystalline with fragments of fossils.

Oolitic limestone is a mass of small calcium carbon spheres created by the forming of calcium carbonate around a nucleus such as a shell fragment. It is comparable to the limescale build-up on the element in kettles in areas where the water is hard. Oolitic limestone provides some of the most well know building stones such as yellow limestone of the Cotswold villages, Portland Stone (a well known example is those used for the portals in the court area of the British Museum) of Dorset, Bath stone and Lincolnshire limestone.

In the south-east of England ragstone, a hard, grey-blue, sandy limestone is often used. It is brittle, difficult to shape and varies a great deal in character. It was used due to the shortage of more suitable stones.

Sandstone

Sandstone is made of the more resistant parts of igneous rocks, essentially fragments of quartz, along with smaller amount of other minerals such as feldspar and mica. The grain size can be large or small, angular or rounded, close together or further apart. By measuring the average size of the grains, sandstones can be divided into fine, medium or coarse-grained types. The key feature of sandstone is that the quartz grains are relatively indestructible, they are harder than limestone, and so can be more resistant to weathering. Sandstone predominates in northern Britain.

Metamorphic rocks

Metamorphic rocks have been altered by heat and pressure so that their chemical and physical appearance is altered to a greater or lesser extent. Limestone becomes marble and shale can become slate, such as that found in the Snowdon area and used for roofing. Coade stone was used extensively in the eighteenth century for mouldings, particularly around doorways.

Marble

Marble is metamorphosed limestone, hard enough to polish, which is not often found in Britain. In the past it has been quarried from Scotland but now the only indigenous marble is from Ledmore, Scotland.

Flint

Flint occurs in chalk as irregular nodules sometime of curious shape. Pieces over 80mm are called cobbles and under 80mm, pebbles. On its own it is a difficult building material so it is often mixed with other materials such as brick, chalk and tiles and plastered over. Flint was very popular in the eighteenth and nineteenth centuries because of its decorative qualities and generally laid in courses with one face of the flint, usually knapped to show the blackness exposed.

Care

Limestone and sandstone are soft and easily worked. Therefore care should be taken when cleaning so that the stone is not marked. Granites, marble and basalts are harder and can be washed easily.

Before washing look for traces of paint – if found do not clean. Do not place near a heat source as if certain stone objects dry too quickly soluble salts inherent within the stone may crystallise and cause the material to fragment.

TEXTILES

Textiles are generally made by weaving threads at right angles, passing alternately over and under each other. The most common materials are wool, silk, cotton, flax and jute. Wool is a type of animal hair from sheep or goat; silk is spun from the cocoon of silkworms; cotton is the fine filaments of fibres produced by the cotton plant after the formation of pods; flax and jute are also taken from plant fibres (hessian sacking is made from jute).

Survival

Textiles do not survive well, with the exception of examples found in waterlogged conditions. It is more common to find textiles adhering to other materials such as metals.

Care

If recovered wet textiles should be kept wet. If recovered dry they should be kept dry. If textiles cannot be fully excavated then keep them within a matrix of their own earth and slightly damp.

If the textile is reasonably stable lay it on a mesh screen and spray gently with a plant sprayer filled with clean or distilled water. To turn the piece over, place another piece of mesh on top of the material and flip the whole thing over to avoid picking up the textile. When lifting make sure the entire piece is supported and keep handling to a minimum.

Store in acid-free materials and use no staples, paper clips or pins. Textiles need a low humidity and good ventilation. Observation should be on-going for insect, bacterial or fungal infections.

If the textile is dry and stable a vacuum cleaner can be used to remove any loose dirt. Make sure a piece of gauze is taped over the nozzle of the vacuum cleaner so no pieces are lost.

If wet, damp blotting paper can be used. Place a light weight on top to soak up the moisture more rapidly.

Dyes

Dyeing is the art of colouring fabrics and other materials. There are three kinds of dyes:

1) natural organic dyes obtained from animal and vegetable sources, e.g. Tyrain purple from Mediterranean shellfish and indigo from plants such as *Indigofera*.
2) mineral dyes, e.g. Prussian blue from cyanide of iron.
3) synthetic dyes, manufactured mostly from coal-tar.

Many dyes are not colour 'fast' or fixed and these will leech out if washed, particularly if subjected to hot water. Do not leave any dyed item in direct sunlight as this will accelerate the loss of colour. This is particularly true of synthetic dyes.

TIN

Tin rarely appears in archaeological contexts in its own right but usually as various alloys, particularly in combination with copper for bronze or copper and lead for pewter. As tin does not tarnish, and is resistant to organic acids, it was used as a protective covering from Roman times onwards. Copper alloy vessels also used tin as a coating to avoid toxicity, this being the case particularly for cooking and serving vessels and utensils.

Identification
A characteristic grey, silvery surface (often covering a metal base). Tin was used in sheet form from the late sixteenth to early seventeenth century in Bohemia. Pontypool, South Wales, became famous for shallow trays decorated with coloured lacquers. Tin sheets were originally hammered over a form, so look for hammer marks. In 1728 sheets were rolled in mills, so look for joins where the sheets meet up.

Survival
Articles of tin are seldom encountered in archaeological sites except from neutral soils.

Clean
Do not get wet if recovered dry, if recovered wet leave to air-dry. When cleaning copper alloy items look for the tin coating in corners and do not wash.

TORTOISESHELL

Tortoiseshell is a misnomer. The shell of the tortoise has been used minimally, in fact it is the turtle shell which has been used and which is known by the term tortoiseshell. It is one of the most widely distributed of all materials and one of its principal uses has been for combs. Tortoiseshell combs were made by hand in England until the 1830s in Yorkshire, the Midlands and Scotland where hundreds were turned out every day. In 1828 comb production became mechanised and mass production saw around 2000 combs a day being made. Tortoiseshell is the horny plates of three types of turtle.

The most common tortoiseshell is the hawksbill from the Caribbean coast, which accounts for most of the western work from Roman times onwards when it was stained to look like wood. The material used comes from the 13 plates on the turtle's carapace which vary in thickness from 0.3cm to 0.7cm depending on the size and age of the turtle – a turtle about 1m long would yield 3.6kg of tortoiseshell. Tortoiseshell was put to a large variety of uses including marquetry, small snuff boxes and particularly combs. The shell has peculiarly 'plastic' properties, which make it so versatile that it can be sawn, or carved (it takes a good polish), easily softened and twisted into shapes, or even tied into knots. It can have metal impressed into it and can be re-used by steaming off the old piece. Tortoiseshell was eventually replaced by plastics.

The green turtle is the second favoured tortoiseshell and was used widely for veneering. It has a greenish reflection and resembles horn more than other tortoiseshell. Green turtle meat is also edible, and was a popular dish – during the eighteenth century it became a passion in London and the arrival of fresh turtle was announced in the *Gentleman's Magazine*. Special inns where turtle was served were given names such as the Ship and Turtle. The loggerhead turtle, found across the Pacific, was often used for fans and cabinet inlay.

Identification
Tortoiseshell is a semi-translucent amber colour mottled with darker brown and red spots, and if from a loggerhead turtle then it may have a greenish hue. It has a glossy lustre and is warm to the touch. Real tortoiseshell fluoresces with a yellow-brown colour in the light of an ultraviolet lamp.

Survival
Tortoiseshell does not survive well in anything but neutral soils.

Care
If found wet, keep wet. If found dry then clean with a soft cloth. The plates on the turtle itself look dull, but once polished and wiped with grease they take on a glossy sheen. This is one of the few artefacts that benefits from being handled as the grease from the hands keeps the tortoiseshell moist. It can warp when near heat so keep away from radiators or any other heat source. It is easily scratched so use no metal tools and store away from other sharp objects.

VENEER

Veneering is the ornamentation of furniture by gluing thin sheets of rarer wood/s (or other materials such as tortoiseshell) to a body of more common wood/s such as pine or oak. This allowed furniture makers to utilise expensive woods more economically and provide more decoration.

Identification
Veneer is found as thin sheets which, when handmade, varied according to the maker. During the eighteenth century veneers were sawn in a saw-press and so had a more uniform thickness of about 16mm. The underside is rough with the front often being highly polished.

Survival
Veneer will have the same survival conditions of wood but due to their thinness will decay more rapidly.

Care
Do not get veneer wet – if dried out too quickly it may warp and split. Veneer by its very nature is thin and fragile so do not leave near a heat source.

WOOD

Wood has been used throughout history for a number of purposes. It is made from bundles of fibres which run lengthwise down the tree. These fibres are well-defined according to species and form the grain. If the fibres are close and compact they are classed as hardwoods, if loosely bound together they are softwood. Wood can be cut with the grain or against the grain and each produces a distinctive pattern. Wood is absorbent and so will take up water.

Wooden
pail

Identification
Wood is usually easily identified. Marks to look for are axe marks, particularly prehistoric flint axes. Hand sawing can be identified by straight lines whereas after around 1800, circular marks can indicate a circular saw. If possible make a measured sketch of any marks – if the wood is allowed to dry out, the evidence for working may disappear so recording of any evidence of marks is essential.

Survival
Dry wood is not often found in Britain but wet wood can survive well in the sea or waterlogged environments, such as old moats or ditches, where the matrix remains damp.

Care
Dry wood should be gently brushed down if it is stable, do not get wet. Wet wood should be kept wet from the moment of exposure. If it is allowed to dry out completely it could lose 90 per cent of its weight and 80 per cent of its volume. It can also warp and crack and if left too long will break apart. Wood can sometimes appear stable but that stability may only extend to a centimetre or so, and the wood underneath can be soft and easily damaged by pressure from fingers. This means indentations can be left when it is pressed.

If wet wood cannot be removed at once from site then cover small items with damp acid-free tissue paper (not newspaper as the print will transfer to the wood). If it is very friable lift the piece directly onto a firm, flat surface such as a board or flat container. Large pieces may need constant spraying or covering with wet bandages, but care should be taken to ensure that the fabric does not snag.

Do not attempt to clean the surface of waterlogged wood as it will simply break apart. Bag up (see page 71) and keep in a dark cool environment, preferably in a bowl or tank filled with water. Monitor the water so that it does not become stagnant.

Waterlogged wood needs to be drawn wet (see page 140) as, if allowed to shrink, an exact record of shape and size could be lost. For stable items wipe them over removing any excess dirt with fingers or a sponge.

7

RECORDING AND MARKING

The standard paperwork used to record archaeological finds has been designed for ease of use and storage. 'Catalogue sheets' are used to record bulk finds, and 'Accession cards' are used for small finds. Formats vary, but most units use forms with pre-printed boxes for completion according to the types of finds present. Always complete the forms in black ball-point ink for clarity of photocopying and scanning. Occasionally it may be necessary to add extra notes – in this event use good quality paper and leave a sufficient margin for file punching. Attach the notes to the forms with plastic-coated paper clips if possible as staples will eventually rust.

If any note has been made on the context label regarding the method of recovery, such as wet sieving or metal detecting, then that information should be carried forward onto the catalogue sheet.

Accession cards
Fill out the card according to the boxes provided. On the back of the card a drawing of the artefact should be included so that if the find becomes separated from its card it can be quickly reunited. If the find cannot be drawn 1:1 then include a scale so the exact size of the item is known. Sketch out the outline (see page 139) and include any diagnostic information. The height, length, width and diameter should be included.

When recording an artefact, note if the condition is unstable so that a record of deterioration can be kept. If any conservation treatment has been applied make a note of this as well.

Marking up
Each artefact recovered from an excavation should eventually be marked, or labelled with a permanent, unique identity reference so that it can be related to its assemblage, context and site. The advantage of 'marking up' is that various finds can be studied together without the risk of them becoming mixed up and losing the context. Even if a number of sherds come from different contexts they should be marked according to context and not to the pot, as it is the contextual data that will provide most information about the movement of the broken pot.

When marking up items avoid writing on:
- uneven surfaces, as they make the writing difficult to read;
- lines of weakness or fracture, as if the piece breaks apart later the number will be cut in half;
- decorated, painted, varnished, pigmented or waxed areas;
- areas that will be visible if the piece is on display;
- areas where abrasion may occur, such as the base on which its rests or where it will be most handled;
- on the side of breaks as the number will be obscured if reconstruction takes place;
- all metals or fragile items which would be damaged by marking them.

Standardise the position of marking as much as possible so that people handling items will know where to look for the marks.

Do not use ink in direct contact with the object as it may become absorbed or stain the surface indelibly. The ink should always be buffered with a base layer of varnish. Do not use other substances as a base layer such as Sellotape, as it has not been designed for longevity. Anyone who has dealt with items on which Sellotape has been used will be familiar with its discolouration and its fragility. Old Sellotape will often break up and pull apart from the surface it was attached to, leaving behind an unsightly brown stain. Correction fluids such as Tippex are also not suitable as their quick drying can cause a lumpy uneven surface which can be difficult to write on without some characters becoming illegible. Correction fluids form an inflexible surface and are subject to cracking and detachment. They are not suitable for long-term storage as they discolour and deteriorate with age and can be hard to remove without leaving a disfiguring white stain.

Prepare the area to be marked by brushing away any dirt – even if the piece has been processed it is often the case that some dirt clings to the surface. Using a good quality small paint brush (cheap brushes will tend to lose hairs) lay down an even, thin layer of a conservation approved varnish such as Paraloid B72 or Paralax. Paraloid B72 is inflammable and should be stored with consideration (it comes in protective tubes), in a well ventilated area and clearly marked with the standard flammable symbol. When it is being used the work place must be well ventilated. If the Paraloid B72 is too thick then use acetone as a thinner. Varnish batches of sherds and allow each batch to dry for five minutes, or until dry. If the brush becomes clogged clean with acetone.

> Paraloid B-72 (also known as Acryloid B-72) is a general-purpose resin much favoured by conservators for a number of jobs. It is durable, non-yellowing and dries to a clear matt transparency. It is also flexible, waterproof and resistant to many alkalis and acids such as grease, vegetable oils and alcohol. It can be used either as a varnish or glue.

Do not use commercially bought clear nail varnish or nail varnish removers as these have been made to a number of formulae, most of which have not been tested with conservation in mind. They are not intended for long-term stability and will become brittle and discoloured with time and some may eat into the fabric of the material being marked. They often contain perfumes and may cause the staining or discolouration of a piece.

> Acetone is a colourless liquid with a characteristic odour of pear drops. It is produced during the dry distillation of wood and other organic bodies. It has many uses including as a varnish thinner and remover. It is flammable so should be stored and used with care.

Using a mapping pen with a suitable nib (such as a Rotring or other similar pen) and the correct ink, write the number on the base layer. Use white ink for dark items and black ink for light ones and write in small but clear lettering. The number should consist of the site code

Masking tape damage

and accession number for small finds, and the site code and sequence of numbers for bulk items. Some organisations encircle the site code and use a diamond shape to enclose the accession number. Wait until the ink is dry, usually about 15 minutes in mild conditions, before applying a second coat of varnish over the number to seal it in. Leave the item to dry for about five minutes before re-bagging. When there are numerous sherds and time is short, the top layer of varnish is often omitted. If the number has to be removed use a cotton bud dipped in acetone and rub lightly over the area.

If a temporary means of marking is needed a small piece of masking tape may be placed over the surface and the number written in. This cannot be a long-term solution as old masking tape will leave a sticky residue if left too long. Do not use masking tape on any surfaces which may flake, or where decoration could be pulled off.

If an item is too small or too fragile to be marked then try to attach a label firmly so that it will remain with the object, but not so tightly that it causes damage. If this is not possible then a label must be kept with it at all times.

For a large item such as statuary, which is to be kept outside, use a conversation approved paint and apply according to the guidelines above. The paint will need to be monitored to check for weathering.

Standard artefact terminology
Code books listing standard artefact terminology are available. There are several such thesauruses including those used by the British Museum or

English Heritage. Whichever code has been adopted by the site managers should be inputted into the site computer(s) to enable statistical
studies to be carried out which will be understood by all parties.

8

ILLUSTRATION

Drawing finds is part of the recording system, even if it is only a sketch on the back of accession cards (see page 131). A drawing can convey more information than a photograph as a photo records only what is before it, whereas an illustration can render decoration in more detail, certain features can be played down in favour of others which may need more study and accurate measurements can be included.

Artefact illustration follows certain conventions which, when understood, enable everyone to read the illustration and gather information from it. An illustration that follows the convention allows no individual quirks and so reduces misinterpretation. The conventions listed here are mainly British and may not conform to standards in other parts of the world. For example, it is traditional here to place the section part of a pottery drawing on the left, whereas in the USA it is placed on the right.

The guidelines supplied here are basic and anyone intending to do extensive archaeological illustrating should refer to the books in the bibliography.

Pencils
Pencils come in 19 varying degrees of hardness of lead but the most useful are those in the middle range. Hard leads can tear the paper and be difficult to erase, and when used too lightly the line can be difficult

to see. A soft lead will look fuller and is easier to erase but can appear blurred in some reproductions, and is more prone to 'wander off' if the pencil is not kept at a steep angle.

Propelling or technical pencils sizes 0.2 to 0.6mm may be preferred as the point is always consistent and no sharpening is required. Sharpen ordinary pencils with a scalpel as a pencil sharpener will sharpen in a uniform manner and to a specific shape. With a scalpel the lead can be sharpened to a finer point than with a sharpener, or shaped to the illustrator's needs.

Pens

Using a variety of pens with different sized nibs allows lines to be produced of varying thickness and removes the need to go over lines. Mapping pens or dipping pens consist of a wooden or plastic handle into which nibs can be inserted. Using these requires practice and inexperienced users often end up with ink all over their fingers. The drawback with these pens is that pressing the nib too hard will cause them to splay and become useless. The most commonly used pens in illustration are the Rotering with an ink cartridge, but these also take time to learn how to use and the nibs can be very sensitive. They require careful looking after and, if left for any length of time, can quickly become clogged up. The main reason for using a cartridge or mapping pen is that the ink is very dark and is excellent for reproduction. If this is not so important, particularly for drawing on accession cards, nylon drawing pens can be bought from any high street stationery shop. These come in a variety of nib sizes and are used by many for quick illustrations.

When using an ink pen, try to produce a smooth and even stroke as, if drawn too slowly, parts of the line may appear thicker than others. This is particularly true of cartridge pens where the ink is freer flowing. If the pen is held at a steep angle it will produce a different thickness of line than if the pen is angled, so try not to alter the angle once drawing has begun.

Ink

Use black and white ink suitable for a mapping or cartridge pen. Always replace the lid when not in use to avoid accidents and drying of the ink. Do not use in conjunction with other pens such as Rotring as it will clog the pens – these require special ink.

Orientation

The first thing that needs to be decided is which way is up and which side needs to be illustrated. In most cases only two drawings for each piece will be needed, the front and a section, unless there are reasons why further sides need to be drawn (such as decorations). Most orientation is obvious and should appear as the piece appears, however this is not always the case. Objects which have a cutting edge such as a stone axe are drawn vertically with the cutting edge at the bottom. This also applies to pointed objects such as needles or swords. Knives, sickles and saws are drawn horizontally with the cutting edge pointing downwards. Arrowheads, and all lithic pointed pieces, are orientated with the point upwards. Prehistoric brooches are drawn horizontally with the foot to the left, but Roman brooches are drawn with the foot pointing downwards.

If there is decoration on the rim or base it will be necessary to show this separately in a side view.

For quick accuracy the outline can be drawn then traced and applied to the other half of the illustration.

The outline

Hold the artefact in the centre of the page or card on a flat surface. If this proves difficult, use plasticine or Blu Tack to lightly secure it. Do not press too hard on the piece, not only to avoid damage, but also because if the plasticine is pressed too hard onto the object removing it may remove parts of the artefact as well. Blu Tack, if left too long, will leave a greasy mark.

Using a pencil, draw around the object. Bear in mind that when tracing free hand around a static item the pencil will have a tendency to change angle, resulting in false measurements. It is necessary to keep the pencil as vertical as possible and use callipers afterwards to determine the exact dimensions. Use only plastic callipers so as not to cause any damage to the artefact – the most useful ones are those with small measuring wheels. Other methods:

- tape the pencil onto a plastic set square and then lightly trace around the item.
- put the set square against the edge and make a dot at the base of the set square. Do this all the way around the object and then join up the dots using a calliper to check the measurements.

- the 'dropped pencil' method where the pencil is placed against the edge and dots made then joined up.
- scan or photocopy the item and then draw in the outlines.
- place a piece of acetate film over the item and trace it, although it can be difficult to hold the film steady and avoid pressing down on the object.

Some people will do a pencil drawing, photocopy it and ink in. This way if there are any errors it can be started again.

Waterlogged items such as wood and leather will need to be drawn using a piece of acetone film and a waterproof pen. Care must be taken not to press down too heavily and break the soft piece. All waterlogged items should be drawn before conservation to gather accurate dimensions, as when dried out they shrink.

The section

Most items are drawn from two angles, the front and the section, which represents the thickness of the object. When moving from one to the other the piece should be rotated 90° to the right.

Measure the thickness of the wall with callipers. With a whole vessel the thickness of wall cannot be ascertained so use dotted lines.

Draw either a short line in the centre between the view of the front and the section or two short lines at the top and bottom. The line should not touch the illustration itself to avoid any confusion. Always include the line if there is more than one item per page, as this will avoid any uncertainty as to which section belongs to which front view.

The section should be filled in solid black or if this appears too much as with large items, use hatching.

Inking in

When the drawing is complete, fill in with black India ink (using a pen or, if there are large areas, a brush may be preferable).

Shading

All shading should be done with a light source coming from over the left shoulder. This means that areas on the left will generally be lighter than areas on the right. Shading is done by using either hatching or stippling. Examine the object to see how the shading appears and represent it by using darker lines or heavier stippling. Stippling can produce a more accurate effect but care needs to be taken not to produce regular dots, but make them random and of different sizes to produce a smooth appearance. Do not let the drawing become too dark as in a reproduction it may appear like a black blob, or if the stippling is too fine it may disappear when photocopied.

Smooth items such as glass and copper alloy surfaces are generally shown with an even stippling and lines, even though there may be corrosion present.

Rough surfaced items such as iron have a more random shading technique used on them with broken lines and stippling.

Colours

Colours are not usually included in an archaeological illustration, but if necessary then a series of hatching and shading can be produced to represent individual colours. If this is done then a key showing which shading represents which colour is required.

Broken objects

If an object is incomplete or broken this is represented by the use of a dotted line to indicate what the illustrator believes the rest of the item would look like. If the illustrator is not sure of the how the remainder of the piece should appear it should not be included.

Mistakes

If a mistake is made once the illustration has been inked up these can be rectified using white correction fluid. Apply evenly so no dark areas appear if the drawing is to be photocopied. It is often easier to use a thin paint brush than the brush supplied in the lid.

Ink can be removed with a scalpel. Use the blade to carefully scrape away the ink without pressing too hard as you may end up cutting the paper. Once the ink has been scraped off use an eraser to smooth down the paper.

Scales

With any scale alongside an illustration the number 1 always refers to the actual size of the object. When represented as 1:1 the drawing is life sized. 2:1 means the drawing is twice the size of the original and 1:2

means it is half the size of the original. Small items should be drawn larger than life so when reduced they do not lose detail.

The inclusion of a scale is important if the illustration is to be reduced for publication it is necessary for the reader to know the original size. The length of the scale should be the same length as the object and should consist of alternate black and white blocks measuring one centimetre each.

References
The site code and accession number should always be included. Instant transferable letters can be used.

Establishing diameters
To establish the diameter of a vessel from a base or rim sherd a radius curve chart is used. A radius chart is a series of concentric lines and can easily be made. Using a pair of compasses draw a series of circles, or half circles, 5mm apart. Generally the smallest should be 2.5cm radius and the largest 15cm. Place the rim or the piece on the line, making sure it fits snugly and there is no space between the rim and the line (wheel thrown vessels give a more accurate reading). Tilting the sherd back and forth often clarifies this. Once the line has been established read the radius size. This will only give the measurement of the rim to the centre of the circle (the radius) so to calculate the diameter then figure has to be doubled.

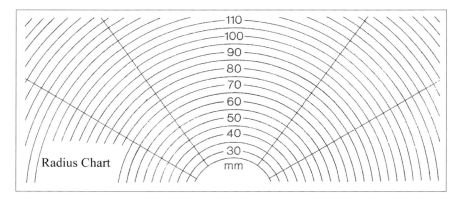

Radius chart

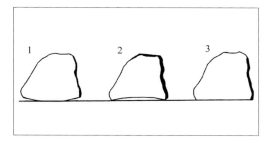

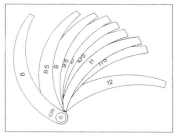

Tilting a sherd   Radius templates

If only a body sherd is present the radius can still be established by using radius templates which can be made quickly out of card. Use a concave template for the exterior and convex for the interior. Alternatively use soldering wire or a French curve (plastic covered wire) pressed lightly around objects and then measure on the radius chart.

Pottery

Pottery is generally drawn in two halves with all the exterior details, such as decoration, shown on the right and interior details and the thickness of the wall shown on the left (in the USA this is reversed). The two sides are divided by a thin vertical line. Along the top is a second line that runs from the central line to both sides but does not touch either the illustration or the section (see below). This is so that details of the rim do not become obscured, particularly when reduced in photocopying. If the pot is wheel-thrown (see page 113) the line is drawn straight using a ruler. If the pot is handmade the line is drawn freehand to indicate its unevenness.

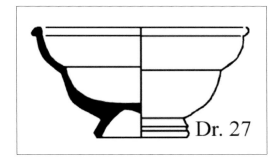

Pot illustration   Section line

As it is rare for a vessel to be recovered complete the sherd can be shown within a series of lines representing the whole pot with the rest of the shape indicated by dotted lines.

If one handle is present it is represented on the right-hand side. If there are two there is one on each side, but the one on the left is done in section. If these are more than two handles, draw them where they appear. If there is decoration on the handle a separate illustration may be necessary. Spouts/lips are normally on the left.

Fingertip impression, especially on the base of a pot, should be shown on the profile side.

If the pot is handmade the section is usually hatched, whilst with wheel-thrown pottery the section is shown as solid black but this is not always adhered to.

Maker's marks and stamps are usually drawn 2:1 to the right-hand side of the drawing.

Lithics

A flint has two sides, the ventral and dorsal. The ventral or front is not often drawn unless there is something significant on it. The dorsal, or back, is most often drawn as it shows the sequence of removals made to create the piece. If both sides are to be included the sequence should be the dorsal, the section then the ventral. The part where the flint is struck, or the proximal end, is place at the bottom of the drawing. The distal, or pointed end, is at the top.

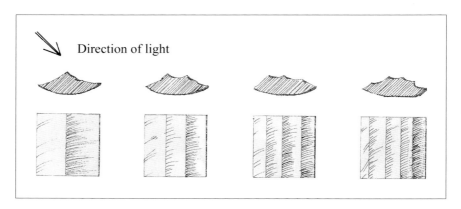

Lithic illustration

The main purpose of lithic drawings is to show the order of flake removal and therefore its order of manufacture. The outline is drawn followed by the main facets which can be drawn in by eye, checking every now and then with the callipers that the distribution is correct. Due to the amount of facets on a flint it is easier to start in pencil and then ink in. When showing the facets, hatched lines should indicate the direction of the blow as well as the depth and angle of the facet. Draw the main lines of the facets with heavier lines and the waves of percussion with lighter lines. If the cortex (outer surface) is present it should be shown with stippling.

9

STORAGE

When storing artefacts for more than a year, or if the artefacts are particularly sensitive, then attention must be given to the relative humidity (RH) levels within the storage area, as the wrong RH can cause artefacts to deteriorate.

RELATIVE HUMIDITY (RH)

Relative humidity is a measure of the amount of water held in a volume of air at a specific temperature, compared to the maximum amount of water that the same volume of air at the same temperature could hold (before it would turn into water droplets such as rain or condensation). RH can vary from 0 to 100 per cent – the damper the air feels the higher the relative humidity, the drier the air feels the lower the relative humidity. For example, if a volume of air is at 20°c with a maximum capacity of 16 grams of water and 16 grams of water is measured, the RH is 100 per cent. If the water measured is 8 grams then the RH is 50 per cent.

Individual artefacts may react differently to the effects of humidity and a composite artefact may have several reactions, depending on the materials within the piece. Where an object is made from elements of the same material, for example a wooden box with inlay of other woods, each part may have a different reaction particularly if it has been made from various sources, or had different treatment. Early adhesives were handmade and so various recipes could react differently.

The time for a reaction to humidity to occur also varies – large items respond more slowly to a new environment, where a life-size wooden piece may take two to three months to stabilise compared to a piece of paper which will react within minutes. Silver tarnish will be accelerated by a high RH and textiles, particularly cotton, linen, wool and silk, will fade.

If the air lacks moisture, items such as wood will dry out and split and paper will become brittle. Drying out often causes a change in shape and size. Organic or moisture containing artefacts should not be left in a RH of below 35-40 per cent for long periods.

Damp air can encourage the growth of moulds and mildew, especially in warm, dark conditions where the RH is above 65-70 per cent. Items attacked by moulds can lose their colour or become mottled and stained. Insects also flourish in a high RH – clothes moths favour a RH of between 20-65/70 per cent and the brown house moth prefers 20-90 per cent RH. Unprotected iron and steel will corrode above a RH of 70 per cent. Generally speaking a RH of 18-21 per cent is recommended although these figures are for guidance only and if in doubt a conservator should be consulted.

Artefact storage spaces should be kept at a consistent RH and it is important that steps, such as installing a humidifier, are taken to retain the levels when the environment is disturbed by an influx of new air. Constantly changing environments can cause organic artefacts to swell, then shrink and so become warped. If allowed to fluctuate too much, the cellular structure of organic artefacts such as bone, ivory and wood could collapse beyond recovery. Maintaining a consistent RH in a room does not completely protect the contents, for if items are left in sunlight they will still be damaged. Sunlight will also raise the temperature of the room, and as the room heats the rising currents of air will collect dust which will then be deposited when cooling.

Controlling the humidity of storage environments will help limit the deterioration of objects and therefore a good understanding of the effects of RH is advisable. There are a number of cheap and simple devices on the market to measure humidity and temperature, and a number of humidifiers can be purchased to maintain an even atmosphere.

Dial hygrometers
This is a simple device for measuring RH, and the type of meter often seen in museum display cabinets. They are cheap, easy to use and reasonably accurate if calibrated correctly.

Thermohygrometers
Also cheap, these are hand-held digital systems to measure RH and temperature of a room or enclosed space. They are small, simple to operate, have an easy-to-read display and run off batteries. They give spot readings only, with accuracy of +/-5 per cent for RH and +/-1-2°c.

ULTRAVIOLET LIGHT

Light can be as equally damaging as humidity, and if not monitored can cause fading, discolouration and brittleness. Light will only affect the area it can reach so most of the damage will be surface deterioration. However as the surface breaks up, light damage will permeate deeper and eventually may compromise the strength of the piece. Unless items are stored in or covered by light-proof protection, the light source should be filtered.

Sunlight is the greatest source of UV and artefacts should be protected from it as much as possible. Windows will magnify the UV content of sunlight to around six times that of a tungsten light.

A standard domestic light bulb is lit from a coiled tungsten filament heated to about 2,700°c, and is a source of UV light. Most of the output from an ordinary light bulb is heat (94 per cent for a 100-watt lamp) and therefore these do not need to be filtered when using to study artefacts. However the heat from the bulb could damage the artefact when placed too close or for a long period of time.

Florescent strip lights emit less UV than daylight and do not produce a great deal of the heat in comparison with a tungsten light bulb. However, they need to be filtered as the UV output is still high enough to damage artefacts.

The simplest method of reducing UV is to purchase ultraviolet absorbing sheets, self-adhesive film or varnish for windows, skylights and any other point of light entry. These will prevent most UV from entering without altering the amount of light, however, they must cover the entire window and they do fade over time and so need to be replaced approximately every three to five years. Strong electric light can also be damaging and filters are available for lamps and strip lights.

Light meters (or lux meters)

Light meters can be used to measure the amount of light present in storage spaces. These are inexpensive battery-operated electronic monitors similar to those used in cameras. They give an immediate light reading and can measure from near darkness to bright light. The ideal light for most items is 50 lux.

EXTERNAL STORAGE

If large items are to be stored outside then they should not sit directly on the ground but on a plinth, to prevent moisture and salts seeping into the piece. Take care to place the piece away from overhanging tree branches to avoid drips of water, leaf sap and bird excrement.

Bronze statuary should be protected with a stable, reversible coating available from conservators.

APPENDIX

MOHS SCALE OF HARDNESS

Some of the materials covered in this book are listed here:

HARDNESS	MINERAL
1	*Talc*
2	*Gypsum*
2.5	*Fingernail*
	Shell
	Alabaster
2.5–3	*Gold and silver*
	Marble
2–3	*Lead*
3	*Calcite*
	Copper penny
	Antler
3.5	*Amber*
	Coral
4	*Fluorite*
	Pearl
4–4.5	*Platinum*
4–5	*Iron*

5	
5.5	*Knife blade*
5–6	*Turquoise*
	Lapis lazuli
6	*Chalk*
6–7	*Glass*
6.5	*Iron pyrites*
	Jade
7	*Quartz*
	Hardened steel
	Basalt
	Limestone
	Amethysts
7–7.5	*Garnets*
7–8	*Granite*
8	*Topaz*
	Emerald
	Aquamarine
9	*Corundum*
	Sapphires
	Rubies
10	*Diamond*

BIBLIOGRAPHY

Adkins, L. & Adkins, R.A. 1989 *Archaeological Illustration*, Cambridge Manuals in
Archaeology, Cambridge University Press

Barham, A.J. & Macphail, R.I. (eds) 1995 *Archaeological Sediments and Soils:
Analysis, Interpretation and Management*, Institute of Archaeology, University
College London, London

Barker, P. 1993 (3rd edition) *Techniques of Archaeological Excavation*, B.T. Batsford,
London

Blinkhorn, P. & Cumberpatch, C.G. in press. The interpretation of artefacts and
the tyranny of the field archaeologist. In *Interpreting Stratigraphy* Proceedings
of the 6th Stratigraphy Conference, Worcester

Brodribb, C. 1970 *Drawing Archaeological Finds for Publication*, John Baker,
London

Collis, J. 2001 *Digging up the Past*, Sutton Publishing, Stroud

Dillon, B.D. (ed.) 1981 The Student's Guide to Archaeological Illustrating,
Archaeological Research Tools, Vol 1, Institute of Archaeology, University of
California, Los Angeles

Dowman, E.A. 1970 *Conservation in Field Archaeology*, Methuen & Co Ltd,
London

Goodyear, F. 1971 *Archaeological Site Science*, Heinemann, London

Greene, K. 2002 (4th Edition) *Archaeology: An Introduction*, Routledge, London

Holliday, V.T. (ed.) 1992 *Soils in Archaeology: Landscape Evolution and Human Occupation*, Smithsonian Institution Press

Hope-Taylor, B. 1966 Archaeological Draughtsmanship: Principles and Practice, Part II, *Antiquity* XL, 107–13

Hope-Taylor, B. 1967 Archaeological Draughtsmanship: Principles and Practice, Part III, *Antiquity* XLI, 181–9

Kenrick, P. 1971 Aids to the Drawing of Finds, *Antiquity* VLV, 205–9

Limbrey, S. 1975 *Soil Science and Archaeology*, Academic Press, London

Maney, A.S. 1980 *The Preparation of Archaeological Illustrations for Reproduction*, Association of Archaeological Illustrators and Surveyors, Technical Paper 1

McCormick, A.G. 1977 A Guide to Archaeological Drawing, *Notes for Students*, Department of Archaeology, Leicester University

Muscarella, O.W. 1984. On publishing unexcavated artifacts, *Journal of Field Archaeology* 11(1): 61–65.

Museum of London 1994 (3rd edition) *Archaeological Site Manual*, Museum of London, London

Piggott, S. 1965 Archaeological Draughtsmanship: Principles and Practice, Part 1, *Antiquity* XXXIX, 165–76

Pye, E. 2001 *Caring for the Past: Issues in Conservation for Archaeology and Museums*, James & James, London

Retallack, G.J. 2001 *Soils of the Past: An Introduction to Paleopedology* Blackwell Science, Oxford

Renfrew, C. & Bahn, P. 2004 (4th edition) *Archaeology: Theories, Methods and Practice*, Thames & Hudson, London

Sease, C.A. *Conservation Manual for the Field Archaeologist*, Archaeological Research Tools, Vol 4, Institute of Archaeology, University of California, Los Angeles

Shackley, M.L. 1975 *Archaeological Sediments: A Survey of Analytical Methods*, Butterworths, London

Schiffer, M. 1976 *Behavioural Archaeology*, Academic Press, New York

Stein, J.K. & Farrand, W.R. 2001 *Sediments in Archaeological Context*, The University of Utah Press, Salt Lake City

INDEX

If you are interested in purchasing other books published by Tempus,
or in case you have difficulty finding any Tempus books in your local bookshop,
you can also place orders directly through our website

www.tempus-publishing.com